INDUSTRIAL GROWTH AND EMPLOYMENT IN INDIA

INDUSTRIAL GROWTH AND EMPLOYMENT IN INDIA

Shoeb Ahmad

KALPAZ PUBLICATIONS
DELHI–110 052

INDUSTRIAL GROWTH AND EMPLOYMENT IN INDIA
(Economics)

Rs. 540

ISBN: 81-7835-218-4

Published in 2004 in India by
Kalpaz Publications
C–30, Satyawati Nagar
Delhi–110 052
E-mail: kalpaz@hotmail.com

Lasertypesetting by: Varsha Graphics, Delhi
Printed at: Mehra Offset Press, Delhi

Dedicated

to

My Parents

Contents

Preface

The term 'Employment' companies in our national economy implicates three major cost components: (i) Input of building materials, (ii) Input of technical, skilled semi-skilled and unskilled labour, and (iii) Overhead costs. In determination of 'employment relationship specifically its opportunity to youths (educated or uneducated) is considered by the simultaneous interaction of socio-economic variable with its contextual factors.

The more important among them are : (a) technology, (b) size of firms, (c) characteristics of product market, (d) behavious of labour supply, (e) operation of government laws, (f) structure of trade unionism, and (g) job relationship and work value.

Keeping in view the perspective outlined above, there has been given reflection on regulated employment holding relationship with industry, welfare and larger question of workers.

The three devices have been confirmed to give light on subject of the study such as; employment opportunities in any industry of the country can be raised through reduction in the unit cost of labour, materials or both.

Employment opportunities in the industry of the country depend on the exploitation of natural resources and the used of advanced technical knowledge.

These two important components inter-play their creation for larger ad complex organisations.

Paradoxically, the source of the industry's resilience are precisely those factors which lead to stagnation in wages productivity and technology these are frame works occupying viability of the building industry. The economic viability of the building industry, in a large measure is due to the vast reserves of the partially employed and unemployed adult men and women from different sectors of the country. With extremely low reservation prices and weak organisational base, which cannot cope with the demands of modern industry, these workers unreluctantly move back and forth between farming and agro-industrial occupations, requiring practically no skills, in response to the fluctuations in demand for labour. As long the vast human resources last, and are sufficiently in excess of the hitherto experienced modest increase in demand for labour in the entire economy, the conditions of subsistence employment will not change.

Farming the entire concept of given subject into six chapters claiming for theoretical and empirical study as made there, opportunities of employment is not found successful unless the industry is simultaneously regulated and casual labour abolished. With the context of such study, analytical study with procured data has been analysed to have concurred results that can make policy frame-work in the present modernised technologies as a motivational device for increasing productivity, earnings and job satisfaction (characterised factors for employment opportunity in our country).

Shoeb Ahmad

1
Introduction

Generation of employment opportunity has been mainly concerned as a major issue since independence of the country for which different plan periods in our country have been symbolically defined so that eradication of poverty and employment situation might be nullified. This concern is even more considerable in the Ninth Plan for growth of labour force for reaching at focal point in the plan period. The period reached a peak level 2.5 per cent per annum in different sectors in order to maintain employment and unemployment situation for great extended coverage of careers of unemployed youth (educated or uneducated, skilled or unskilled) in segregated occupational departments existing in the country. Such absorption of the youth (male or female) emerges pattern of employment depending upon policy measures continuing from preceding plan periods of the country.

This continuation of employment opportunity in various sectors, particularly industrial sectors relating to knowledge and understanding of issues at various levels in framework for development of growth of employment indicates totality in employment opportunity. This opportunity shows greater contribution for finding healthy growths to economic, social and economic aspects that have been generated since independence. In the post-independence of the country, there strengthened approached labour force in the industrial sectors of the country for solving the serious problems, i.e., employment consideration to the individuals of the population of the country.

The strategy of planned industrialization attributed peaceful climate for industrial relations dealing with great enthusiasm and significant influences undertaken into determination of Indian industry subject to the condition of the following: production function framework for analyzing productivity trends, sharing of productivity gains, and share of labour in industrial and national product. These ingredients show significance of earnings classified into occupations of persons indulged in different factors such as explanation of wages, occupations and regions, etc., usually known as explanatory variables.

An important feature of the employment situation in India has been that the rates of unemployment are rather low, and they have been so overtime. Even if we make a reasonable estimate of underemployment and add it to the rates of unemployment, the overall rate of unemployment will still be what could be described as 'low' for an underdeveloped economy where one third of the population is counted among those living below a modestly defined poverty line. This largely because, as has been observed earlier by many who have dealt with the issue, the 'poor cannot afford to live without work'. But this has also been possible because India has, overtime, sustained an economic structure, which makes it possible for people to create work for themselves, even if it is at low levels of income. If these features of the economic structure change, there will be more open unemployment.

Low unemployment rates have existed with high levels of poverty. This has raised the debate about visible and invisible underemployment resulting in low levels of income. There will be made argument that income and employment have to be considered as two different phenomena. Employment with low income should not automatically means underemployment. Underemployment should only be measured with reference to time disposition, while income from employment may indicate quality of employment, while the aim should be to constantly improve the quality of employment, employment even with low income is preferable to absolute unemployment, since unemployment leads to 'exclusion' from social and economic mainstream and a high rate of unemployment could become a source of acute social tension.

A feature, which is seen to be emerging more sharply, now than earlier, is that more among the openly unemployed are non-poor. Also, more among the openly unemployed are educated. This has implications for the nature of the efforts required to generate additional work opportunities for the unemployed.

Trends in Employment and Unemployment

Comprehensive and comparable estimates of the employment and unemployment situation in the country are available from the surveys carried out by the National Sample Survey Organization (NSSO) on a quinquennial basis. These surveys also produce data on household consumption expenditure on the basis of which the incidence of poverty is estimated. From 1972-73 to 1993-94 , five rounds of quinquennial surveys have been completed. Some social tabulations of 1993-94 round of survey were obtained to help to analyze the employment situation for the preparation of the Ninth Plan. The chapter on employment Perspective in the Ninth Five Year Pan document presents a detailed analysis of the employment situation based on largely on NSS data, and also the data tabulated in the Planning Commission.

Table 1.1 presents the rates of growth of employment and labour force during the interquinquennial periods from 1972-73 to 1993-94. The rates of growth of employment on usual status basis during the four inter-qinquennial periods have varied between 1.6 per cent per annum to 2.7 per cent per annum, and the labour force growth in the corresponding periods has been in the range of 1.8 per cent to 2.9 per cent per annum. In spite of period specific differences in the rates of employment growth vis-à-vis the rates of labour force growth, on the whole over the longer period, the employment growth has kept pace with the growth in labour force without producing a clear trend in the rates of unemployment (on usual status basis) over this longer period.

Table 1.1

Rates of Growth of Employment and Labour Force

(Per Cent Per Annum)

Period	*Rate of Growth of Employment (Usual Status)*	*Rate of Growth of Labour Force*
1972-73 to 11977-78	2.73	2.94
1977-78 to 1983	2.13	2.00
1983 to 1987-88	1.58	1.78
1987-88 to 1993-94	2.43	2.29
1993-94 to 1999-2000	2.89	2.63

Source: National Sample Survey Organisation (NSSO) Quinquennial basis.

Further, infering growth rate of employment and labour force, the discussions of unemployment rates (rural-urban location) in respect of classified gender in India as:

Panel A: Current Daily Status Unemployment Rates

Period	Rural		Urban	
	Male	Female	Male	Female
1993-94	56	56	67	105
1999-2000	72	68	72	96
2000-2001	76	73	78	103

Panel B: Usual Status Unemployment Rates for the Educated

Period	Secondary and above		Graduate and above	
	Male	Female	Male	Female
1993-94 (R)	89	243	134	323
(U)	69	207	64	203
1999-2000 (R)	69	204	107	351
(U)	66	163	66	163
2000-2001 (R)	73	208	109	355
(U)	70	169	71	68

Note: R – Rural, U- Urban.

Source: Economic and Political Weekly, March 17, 2001, p. 935 workforce with respect to industry division in India (1993-94).

Workforce With Respect To Industry Division 1999-00

(in '000')

Classified industry	1999-2000	2000-2001
1 agriculture & allied activities	239096	234293
2 Missing & quarrying	2681	2157
3 283 Manufacturing	39914	44782
4 Electricity, gas & water	1396	1011
5 Construction	12147	18333
6 Trade, Hotels and communication	28502	41325
7 Activity	374390	397,272

Source : Economic and Political Weekly, March 17, 2001, p. 935.

Employment Situation Prevailing to the Organized Manufacturing Sectors in India

In fact, the employment situation to the organized sectors in India showed stagnant conditions during 1980s but it grew in the 1990s as provided in the analysis of data conducted by Annual Survey of Industries (ASI). The ASI has studied employment situation in India for the organized manufacturing industries. This survey published by central statistical organizations, Department of Statistics, Ministry of Planning and Programming evaluated coverage of all factories under sections 2m (i) and 2 m (ii) of the factories Act, 1948 showed the following investigations :

(i) Between 1980-81 and 1990-91, employment in organized manufacturing sectors growth = 0.53% p.a.

(ii) Between 1990-91 to 1995-96, employment in organized manufacturing sectors growth = 4.03% p.a.

The period 1990s showed significant results for employment considerations and found more favourable. For the growth during 1970 (about 3.8 per cent p.a. in making evaluation, the period 1990-91 to 1997-98, the growth rate of employment in organised manufacturing sectors followed 2.69 per cent p.a. for considering the following issues such as;

(a) Greater labour market flexibility; and

(b) Increased trade orientation following intensive industries and techniques of production.

Thus the new labour economic policy evidenced increased competition on the hand and greatly improved access to foreign technology and imported capitals on the other. These two important factors have led to increasing capital intensity that made favourable effects of economic reforms in case of industrial employment.

Though various studies conducted by several authors (Mundle 1992; 1993, Deshpande 1992; Bhattacharya and Mitra 1993; Mitra 1993, Agarwal and Goldar 1995; and Kundu (1997) resulted that the employment situation in industrial fields of the country as pessimistic in the post-reform period. Such remarks might be conceived and proven wing in sense of accelerated growth of employment to the organized manufacturing sectors of the country.

In view of such suspected amount of information the following tables 1.1. and 1.2 show a comparison of employment growth rate between public sector and private sector (including joint sector) factories for three periods: 1973-74 to 1980-81 to 1990-91 and 1990-91 to 1977-98 shown below:

Table 1.1
Distribution for Employment in Organised Industries of India for Period 1973-1998

Sector	*Employment (000)*					
	1973-74	*1980-81*	*1990-91*	*1997-98*	*1999-2000*	*2000-01 (Projected*
Public	1365	2049	2121	3388	3182	3193
Private joint (including unspecified)	4455	5666	5839	7518	7743	7932
Aggregate ASI (including electricity)	5820	7715	8163	8126	10925	11125

Source : Annual Survey of Industries (ASI).

Table 1.2 presents the rates of unemployment according to three different methods of measuring employment/unemployment, i.e. the usual status basis (US), the current weekly status basis (CWS) and the current daily status (CDS) basis. Unemployment rates on usual status basis have ranged between 1.61 per cent to 2.62 per cent without a clear trend over the period 1972-1993. Unemployment rates on CWS basis showed a mildly increasing trend till 1987, and then declined to 3.63 per cent in 1993. On CDS basis there is declining trend of unemployment. Since the current daily status basis of measuring unemployment is closest to measuring unemployment by person days of work, a declining trend in unemployment rates on this basis would mean that the per capita availability of work has increased over the years, or the extent of underemployment has gone down.

Table 1.2

Unemployment Rates

Year	*Usual Status (US)*	*CurrentWeekly Status (CWS)*	*Current daily Status (CDS)*
1972-73	1.61	4.32	8.35
977-78	2.47	4.48	8.18
1983	1.90	4.51	8.28
1987-88	2.62	4.80	6.09
1993-94	1.90	3.63	6.03
1999-2000	2.32	3.89	7.02

Source: Same as previous table, Annual Survey of Industries (ASI).

Also, in estimating per 1,00 distribution of adult (15 and above) usually working persons (principal and subsidiary) who had sought or were available for additional work by gender and rural urban location in India, 1993-94 and 1999-2000, the following tabular form is shown as below:

There exist wide differences between rural and urban areas in respect of the overall incidence of unemployment. As can be seen from Table below 1.3, the person days unemployment rates in urban areas have been consistently higher than in the rural areas. Though the person days unemployment rate (CDS) has shown a decline over the years, the decline is sharper in the rural areas than in the urban areas. The reasons for this may be that the rural areas provide more opportunities of self-employment. And for the same reason employment in rural areas may hide a higher degree of underemployment also.

Category	1993-94 Sought		1999-2000 Sought	
	Most Days	Some Days	Most Days	Some days
Rural Males				
Self-employed	28 (8)	30 (11)	28 (10)	47 (20)
Casual Labourers	44 (15)	69 (27)	71 (21)	99 (46)
All Workers	29 (9)	42 (16)	43 (14)	64 (28)
Rural Females				
Self-employed	12 (5)	20 (8)	20 (5)	23 (10)
Casual Labourers	35 (13)	53 (21)	47 (19)	79 (35)
All Workers	22 (8)	33 (12)	31 (11)	45 (20)
Urban Males				
Self-employed	23 (11)	19 (8)	24 (11)	37 (15)
Casual Labourers	55 (21)	55 (18)	53 (18)	86 (38)
All Workers	24 (9)	21 (7)	25 (10)	37 (15)
Urban Females				
Self-employed	23 (10)	24 (10)	24 (10)	33 (15)
Casual Labourer	47 (19)	50 (12)	46 (13)	70 (23)
All Workers	29 (11)	26 (8)	27 (10)	34 (10)

Source: Compiled from collected information based on National sample survey organisation.

Note: Projected values for 2000-01 & 2001-02 from given instructions.

There exist wide differences between rural and urban areas in respect of the overall incidence of unemployment. As can be seen from Table below the person days unemployment rates in urban areas have been consistently higher than in the rural areas. Though the person days unemployment rate (CDS) has shown a decline over the years, the decline is sharper in the rural areas than in the urban areas. The reasons for this may be that the rural areas provide more opportunities of self-employment. And for the same reason employment in rural areas may hide a higher degree of underemployent also.

Unemployment Rates in Rural and Urban Areas

(Current daily status)

Year	Rural	Urban
1972-73	8.21	8.99
1977-78	7.70	10.34
1983	5.94	9.52
1987-88	5.25	9.36
1993-94	5.63	7.43
1999-2000	6.69	8.20
2000-2001 (Projected)	6.93	8.91

Source: Based on NSSO.

In this way, activity status (principal + Subsidiary) of workers for both males and females in rural and urban areas has been estimated for periods 1993-94 and 1999-2000 as per 1000 distribution

Activity Status	*Rural Males*		*Rural Females*		*Urban Males*		*Urban Females*	
	1993-1994	1999-2000	1993-1994	1999-2000	1993-1994	1999-2000	1993-1994	1999 2000
Unemployed		15	19	11	15	10	10	98
Outside labour force		19	19	112	103	911	76	68

Source: Based on NSSO.

Underemployment

Underemployment signify for partial employment indicating not full work. In other words, the person unemployed for part of the time he/she offers for work. That means to say, the person unemployed for part of the time he/she is in the labour force. The extent of underemployment, thus, could be estimated with reference to the disposition of offered labour time between work and nonwork. The underemployment of those considered or classified as 'employed' exists because a person is considered working if he/she is engaged for a relatively longer time during the reference.

Further, table 1.2 presents (percent per Annum) for growth rate of employment in the organised industries of India following private and public sectors for three mentioned periods as indicated in the table.

Distribution of Table 1.2 growth rates of employment in organised industries (private and public sectors).

Sector	*Growth rate (% p.a)*		
	1973-80	1980-90	1990-97
Public	5.971	1.265	0.391
Private and Joint	3.495	0.302	3.715
Aggregate ASI	4.108	0.566	2.834

Source : Same as in table 1.1.

Again, growth rate of employment for males and females in following activities has been estimated (1993-94) and (1999-2000) as;

(% p a)

	Males	Females
1. Public Work	3.83	5.04
2. Casual Labour in agricultures	2.80	2.94
3. Casual labour in non-agriculture	3.70	5.07
4. Casual labour in all activities	3.59	3.19

Source: NSSO : 1996, 2000.

The tables 1.1 and 1.2 are found that in the 1970s employment grew rapidly in both public and private sector factories. There was a sharp declaration in employment growth in the 1980s in both sectors. But in 1990s, the growth rate of employment in public sector factories has come down further. It was only 0.4 per cent per annum between 1990-91 and 1997-98. By contrast, the growth rate of employment in private sector factories has recovered and surpassed the growth rate prevailing in the 1970s with consequence that almost the entire increase in employment in organized manufacturing industries of the country that taken place in the 1990 is accounted for by the private sector factories.

Also, an interest has been laid that the following tables 1.4 and 1.5 show the size structure of factories (classified into 0-49, 50-99. . . .2000-4999 and 5000) that provided distribution of employment-(%) as well as growth rate (%, p.a.).

The table 1.3 provides labour intensive in the lower size of factories that indicates favourable effect on employment than the higher size of factories (as 5000 +) due to reason of most capital intensive.

Again, there is followed growth rate of distribution of employment accorded to factory size as given in the table 1.4.

Table 1.3
Distribution of Employment by Factory Size

Size	*Distribution of Employment*					
	1973-74	1980-81	1990-91	1997-98	1999-200	2000-2001 (Projected)
0-4	14.4	13.8	17.5	16.8	15.3	15.4
50-99	8.2	9.0	10.8	13.1	14.2	14.9
100-199	9.4	9.2	10.7	12.9	13.2	12.7
200-499	13.1	12.1	13.5	19.0	20.1	10.3
500-999	11.6	9.7	12.0	13.6	14.2	14.7
1000-1999	12.8	13.7	10.1	9.4	10.3	10.9
2000-4999	16.7	15.9	9.5	10.0	10.4	11.2
5000+	13.8	16.6	15.9	5.2	2.3	9.9
Total	100.0	100.0	100.0	100.0	100.0	100.0

Source : Same as Table 1.1.

However, the two above mentioned tables 1.3 and 1.4 reflect that there is sharp decline in the relative share of the size class 5000+ in the 1990s and the increase in the relative share of size classes 50-99, 100-199,and 200-499 must have made a significant contribution to employment growth in this period.

Table 1.4
Distribution of Growth Rate of Employment Situation to the Organised Manufacturing Sectors of India

Size	*Growth Rate (per cent per annum)*			
	1973-80	*1980-90*	*1990-97*	*2000-2001 (Projected)*
0-49	3.477	2.983	2.201	2.103
0-99	5.502	2.416	5.686	5.987
100-199	3.789	2.096	5.652	5.732
200-499	2.934	1.673	7.979	7.993
500-999	1.481	2.729	4.711	4.821
1000-1999	5.124	-2.454	1.815	1.932
2000-4999	3.381	-4.482	3.649	3.864
5000+	6.892	0.134	-12.438	1.543
Total	4.108	0.566	2.835	2.953

Source : Same as Table 1.1.

Remarks

In this context, the economic policy regime has a major influence on the size structure of industries. In the early 1960s, factory employment was heavily concentrated in very large establishment. (Little 1986). During the period the share of small and medium size factories resulted small following imbalanced employment situation in factories. This imbalance in the structure of the manufacturing sector was largely a consequence of the economic policies of the government.

The same author Little (1986) has also commented that protection, investment incentives, credit control and the promotion of industry in the public sector discriminated against the small investment and favoured capital – intensive, large scale establishments. The change in the size structure that has taken place in the 1980s and 1990s a decline in the relative share by big units and a rise in the share of small and medium size factories.

Thus, it has been observed by studying tables 1.3 and 1.4, the structure in employment situation to the manufacturing industries of the country has taken place in the 1980s and 1990s, a decline in the relative share of big units and arise in the share of small and medium size factories, is arguably a correction of the structural imbalance prevailing earlier. But such prevalence has been eliminated in the process of manufacturing industries by means of making correction in very consequent manner to maintaining imbalanced growth of employment considerations. This change is consisted with changes in economic policy, especially the liberalization of industrial and trade policies.

Further, for declined position of employment growth in 1980s compared to 1990s, a study relating to two digit industries has been made in measures of employment growth rate and gross value added to the two digit industries for periods 1980-90 and 1990-97 as presented in the following table 1.5.

Table 1.5

Growth Rates in Employment and Gross Value Added: Two Digit Industries

(percent per annum)

Industry Code	*Employment Growth Rate*		*Real Gross Value Added Growth rate*		
	1980-90	1990-97	1980-90	1990-97	2000-2001 (Projected)
20-21	-1.58	2.70	12.03	7.39	7.47
22	3.71	2.95	8.48	7.83	7.95
23	-3.17	0.58	2.63	0.26	0.32
24	3.02	2.67	13.79	8.35	8.93
25	-3.00	1.06	-4.34	6.56	6.93
26	5.62	1.37	14.63	0.44	0.49
27	-1.79	1.80	5.71	-6.74	6.95
28	0.45	2.30	5.54	3.54	4.02
29	5.91	2.24	11.67	10.46	10.92
30	1.16	5.22	10.30	9.83	9.94
31	3.73	4.72	14.31	5.82	5.93
32	2.03	0.30	11.54	4.29	4.44
33	0.73	0.91	6.55	11.15	11.34

34	1.58	2.83	8.06	9.98	9.99
35+36+39	3.54	2.56	8.62	7.21	7.43
37	-0.18	2.10	7.13	9.39	9.43
38	2.81	7.14	.96	18.98	18.99
Manufacturing	0.53	2.69	8.67	7.43	7.47

Source: Same as in table 1.1.

Note Two-digit industry codes:

20-21	food products;
22	Beverages, tobacco;
23	Cotton textile;
24	Wool, silk, man-made fibred textiles;
25	Jute and other textiles;
26	Textile products;
27	Wood and wood products;
28	Paper and paper products;
29	Leather and Leather products;
30	Chemical and Chemical Products;
31	Rubber, plastic and chemical products;
32	Non-melatic mineral products;
33	Basic metals and alloys;
34	Metal products and parts;
35-36	Machinery and equipment;
37.	Transport equipment
38.	Other manufacturing industries; and
39.	Repair of capital goods.

The figures presented in above-mentioned table 1.5 showed that these industries are labour intensive and accounted for 41 percent of total organized manufacturing employment in 1980. In all these case, the downward trend in employment was arrested in the 1990s and reversed.

Source: ASI.

Furthermore, a study relating growth rates of real wages and man-day per employee has been evaluated corresponding to coded industries. This study focuses considerable emphasis on the increase in man days per employee as a cause of sluggish employment growth in manufacturing industries of the country to know the trend of employment opportunities for two assumed mentioned periods 1980-90 and 1990-97.

In context of this study, Nagaraj (1994) and Bhalotra (1998) have laid considerable emphasis on the increase in man days per employee. This study was to know the remark on employment situation. The data relating to relating wages growth rate and manday per employee growth rate for periods in per cent per annum have been undertaken into consideration the following table 1.6 corresponding to two digits – industries to assess an acceleration in employment growth or stagnation in the different industries of India.

Table 1.6

Distribution of Growth Rates of Real Wages and Manday Per Employee : Two-digit Industries

Industry (Code)	Real Wages Growth Rate		Man day per employee Growth Rate		
	1880-1990	1990-97	1980-90	1990-97	2000-2001
20-21	10.74	1.75	5.24	0.59	0.67
22	2.17	1.61	0.47	0.75	0.83
23	3.64	-.61	0.72	-0.11	0.19
24	6.26	3.32	0.41	-0.09	0.10
25	1.42	4.38	0.30	-0.44	0.67
26	3.25	0.77	0.26	-0.05	0.08
27	4.90	-7.29	0.54	0.56	0.65
28	2.48	3.29	0.34	0.00	0.03
29	0.35	6.38	0.15	0.05	0.09
30	6.70	1.04	0.79	0.00	0.00
31	3.93	5.04	1.03	0.19	0.20
32	2.56	3.53	-0.15	1.39	1.47
33	1.47	5.12	0.33	-0.20	0.31
34	0.76	5.08	0.29	0.31	0.42
35+36+39	-4.17	3.04	0.38	0.05	0.07

37	4.10	5.64	0.21	-0.40	0.51
38	7.83	5.95	-0.36	-0.37	0.42
Manufacturing	4.84	2.48	1.11	0.14	0.15

Note : Two digit industry codes indicating same manufactured products as explained in Table 1.5. But the availability of data for 1997-98 is not existing there.
Source: ASI

The evaluated study in table 1.6 shows the growth rates in real wages (product wage) and man days per employee that might have explained accelerated and stagnated trend for employment situation in the country. The study emphasis the growth because the rate of real wages in aggregate manufacturing growth because the rate of real wages in aggregate manufacturing growth shows the real wages in aggregate manufacturing declined significantly in the 1990s, this occurred also in a majority of industries. Further, looking at the inter-industry pattern of changes in rates of growth in employment and real wages, an inverse relationship can be seen between the two : the extent of acceleration in employment growth is generally higher in those industries in which there has been a greater decline in the growth rate of real wages.

The study performed in the table 1.6 also revealed that at the aggregate level, the rate of increase in man days per employee was 1.11 percent per annum, which, to a large extent was due to the increase that took place in food products industry. Thus, it seems that Nagaraj (1994) and Bhalotra (1998) have commented undue emphasis on assigned factor – a cause of jobless industrial growth in the 1980s. The tables 1.6 provide the change in the growth rate of man-days per employee between two periods in small for most industries and therefore this cannot be major cause of the acceleration in employment growth in the 1990s.

The problem relating to uprising trend of employment opportunities in the light of industrial development is to be examined at a rate commensurating with the growth of industrial output and investment and also invariable factors involved in this behaviour. The behaviour for provision of larger consideration of employment opportunity to the people of India stands as the corner-stone of employment policy by analyzing spatial or locational scales. The scales regarding to employment policy of the different plans, special adaptations and shift of emphasis etc. have been used to admit certain special situations.

In our country, the specification of stated ingredients have mainly considered in our different Five-Year Plan periods stressing on certain measures being undertaken with employment policy through greater and economic development of the country. It is true that planning in India is undergoing a sea change for large masses of the people of the country, who are involved in the vicious circle of poverty, whether in rural or urban sectors. To achieve the objective of economic equality and social justice, it is necessary to sharp out poverty.

Again reflecting on employment situation, there is considered the nature of employment into two forms, namely usual status and current daily status. The first classified employment does not make any indication of unemployment situation. But the second classified nature of employment provides the concept of underemployment to the persons of the country.

In this regard, NSS (National Sample Survey, 1993-1994) have collected information's about persons employed (weekly status) to males and females for both sectors rural and urban of the country by considering days worked in a week, in an indication of per thousand of employment as provided in the following table 1.7. The table has provided data collected information's based on time disposition of the labour force emerging the level of income and consumption between employer and employee.

Further, an investigation has been made for giving reflection in determination of two important factors, namely 'unemployment' and 'poverty' for selected states of the country in indication of current daily status unemployment rates as well incidence of poverty following the period 1993-94. In light of this investigation the following table 1.8 based in NSS data has been used in resultant of employment rates (%) and head count ratio (%). In this context, the table 19 concentrates the percentage of incidence of poverty among employed and unemployed persons of the country since 1977-94 has been estimated following the percentge of persons below the poverty line among the unemployed which is found smaller than among employed.

The current weekly status may be reflected from data obtained by NSS (1993-94) considering rural and urban sectors of the country enlightening 'days worked in a week' as show in the following table 1.7.

Table 1.7

Persons Employed According To Current Weekly Status Concept Distributed By Number Of Days Worked In A Week

Days worked	Rural		Urban		All Areas		
in a week	Male	Female	Male	Female	Male	Female	Persons
0.5-1.0	5	11	3	14	5	12	7
1.5-3,0	28	87	14	59	26	84	44
3.5-5.0	67	246	37	183	62	239	118
5.5-6.0	27	36	35	38	29	36	31
6.5-7.0	873	620	911	706	878	629	800
All	1000	1000	1000	1000	1000	1000	1000

Source NSS data, 1993-94.

However, irrespective of the reason for seeking additional work, the fact that they were seeking additional work (were in the labour market) and did get this additional work, we may count all of these 6.1 per cent of UWP as underemployed. However, we have to still convert this underemployment into its unemployment equivalent. Following the assumption that unemployment is equivalent to half the underemployment, we may add 3.05 per cent to the rate of unemployment on usual status basis to get3.05 + 1.90=4.95 or nearly 5 per cent. Thus, according to this calculation unemployment, taking into account underemployment in 1993-94, would have been about 5 per cent.

The distribution of usually employed persons classified by their current weekly status which is explained in the following tables 1.8 and 1.9 as shown below. In the year 1993-94, 8.6 per cent of the usually employed persons were out of work. Out of these 7.2 per cent were out of work because they had withdrawn from the labour force. Only the remaining 1.4 per cent were unemployed, though seeking work. If we add these 1.4 per cent unemployed to the figure of 1.9 per cent unemployed on usual status basis, we get figure of 3.3 per cent who could be considered to be unemployed taking into account the underemployment which might have shown in the tabular form as:

Table 1.8
Unemployment Rate (Usual Status) Among The Educated (Secndary Education Plus) Youth (Age 15 Plus)

	Unemployment	Per cent share in total unemployed
1977-78	15.4	28.8
1983	11.3	43.7
1987-88	11.8	39.9
1993-94	9.6	62.0
1996-97 (Projected)	7.3	67.0

Source: Information Based on National Sample Survey Organisation.

Thus total unemployment, taking into account the underemployment, would be in the range of 3.3 per cent on the lower side and 6.13 per cent on the higher side. The higher figure being almost the estimate of unemployment on current daily status basis. It may also be seen that the rate of underemployment over the years has been declining.

Table 1.9
Usually Employed Persons Classified by their Current Weekly Status: 1983-2002

Per thousand of the usually employed persons

Activity according to current week.atus	1983	1987-88	1993-94	2001-02 (Projected)
Employed	844	854	914	819
Out of work, due to being:	156	146	86	79
Unemployed	22	17	14	10
Not in labour force	133	128	72	92
All the usually employed	1000	1000	1000	1000

Table 1.10
Incidence of Poverty by Nature of Employment

Nature of work	Rural poverty ratio (per cent)	Nature of work	Urban poverty ratio (per cent)
Self-employed in agriculture	29.05	Self employed	34.68
Self employed in	31.95	Casual labour	61.80

non-agriculture			
Agriculture labour	56.78	Regular wage/ salary earner	20.35
Other labour	39.60	Other households	27.85
Other households	22.48		

Source : Based on NSS data.

As expected, in urban areas the regular wage/salary earners have the lowest incidence of poverty. Bearing the category of other households (where the nature of work is not clear), the self-employed in agriculture have the lowest incidence of poverty in rural areas, even lower than the self-employed in urban areas. This is because of the self-employed in agriculture own land and ownership of assets, particularly land, is an important factor in mitigating poverty.

Educated Employment

The incidence of unemployment among the educated is very high. In 1993-94, it was 9.6 per cent as against the overall unemployment rate of 1.9 per cent on usual status basis. While the incidence of unemployment among the educated has shown a decreasing trend over the period, 1977-78 to 1993-94. The share of the educated among the unemployed has risen during this period. The decline in the incidence of unemployment among the educated means faster growth in educated employment as compared to the growth the educated means faster growth in educated employment as compared to the growth in the educated labour force. The rate of growth in employment among the educated during the reference period, i.e., 1977-78 to 1993-94, has been higher than the overall growth of employment. On the other hand, the Labour Force Participation Rate (LFPR) among the educated decided by approximately percent points during this period. The decline in the LFPR among the educated can be explained by the expansion in the avenues of higher education for younger persons over 15 years of age. Rising share of educated among the unemployed may be a reflection of the unwillingness on the part of the educated to accept low-income jobs.

Policy Implications

From the analysis of the data on the classification of workers by nature of employment and rates of labour participation and those of employment and unemployment by different concepts, it may be summarised that relatively low levels of unemployment rates in India are rooted in the economic structure that has been maintained overtime. The main contribution of this structure appears to have been that it has rendered opportunities for self-employment and also maintained high labour intensity of economic activities. In the rural areas this structure is mainly characterized by widely dispersed ownership of land, even though this amounts to small operational holdings. Marginal and small holdings account for the 78 per cent of operational holdings and nearly one-third of the land cultivated, where the average size is 0.95 hectares. This accounts for a fairly large proportion of workers in rural areas to be self-employed in agriculture. Self-employed in agriculture consistitutes about 38 per cent of the rural workers' households. Another large category of workers' households in rural areas is agricultural labourers accounting for over 30 per cent of the workers. Absorption of such large workforce in agriculture has been possible because of highly labour intensive agriculture based on peasant farming system. Any radical change in the land distribution pattern and the nature of farm operation like large-scale commercial farming would render a very large proportion of these workers completely unemployed. It is a positive aspect of agricultural structure that it has significantly contributed to growth and to the achievement of goals of food security. This structure has also lent stability to the system. As a matter of policy we have to sustain this structure of production and make constant efforts to encourage investment in agriculture and improve productivity.

In the urban sector about one-third of the workers' households belong to the category of self-employed households whereas about a little more than 13 per cent belong to the category of casual labour households. It has also been seen that self-employed workers in urban areas do somewhat better in terms of average earnings than the casual workers. It has been possible for such a large proportion of workers to be self-employed in urban areas because of the existence of the informal sector. In view of this, our approach and policies towards the informal sector acquire significance. Though all the unemployed may not be poor, yet for the poor the only solution to poverty is employment with reasonable income. Such employment is not going to be generated at a large-scale in the organised sector in the near future. All efforts are needed to integrate the informal activities in the mainstream of economic activities in urban areas providing space and facilities for such activities as well as efforts to upgrade the productivity in the informal sector.

It is to be noted an emerging trend that more among the unemployed are non-poor and also more among the unemployed are educated. In the past the overwhelming emphasis on the part of the state has been to create additional work opportunities for the most unskilled type of workers, i.e., work opportunities in earth work and construction etc. There has been limited programmes to assist the educated urban youth by way of subsidized investment loan to help them get into some remunerative economic activity. But administered as they are through a machinery with different layers of command and control system, difficulties in making a choice of the more promising candidates and leakages at various points, etc., had made these programmes also less successful. I think we will have to move from a direct subsidy type of incentive to make efforts in creating an infrastructure and a supportive environment for self employment for the educated. A big thrust, in this context, on promoting information technology and creating the right type of infrastructure and supportive environment for this is a move in the right direction. One could think of systematic promotion of many other service oriented activities for self-employment of the educated unemployed.

The overall approach in the Ninth Plan (1997-2002) towards employment generation is that the employment should be generated in the growth process itself by concentrating on sectors, sub-sectors and technologies which are more labour intensive in regions characterized by higher rates of unemployment and underemployment. The ninth plan proposes to follow region specific programmes and policies for employment keeping in view the wise differences in the prevailing situation and potential of different states. Towards this end, the Ninth Plan will reinforce the strategies of the Eighth Plan and will put greater emphasis on agricultural growth, growth of small industries, and creation of self-employment opportunities. Overall, growth will be maintained by special emphasis on building up infrastructure, information technology and economic reforms. Also, the special employment progrmmes are sought to be given a sharp regional focus for making them more effective in achieving the objective of ameliorating the condition of the distressed. The Employment Assurance Programme has been strengthened and universalised to cover the entire country.

For development of planning in India, there exist two important issues, Viz ; Poverty alleviation and employment generation, all these two components received greater and more extended attention during the last two decades and a half. The achievement emphsised 'labour force' - covering gainful activity regularly and occasionally and also seeking or available for work. In this context, there was determined labour force 37.4 per cent of the total population resulting 18.7 million persons remaining unemployed as on March 1995, accounting for 5.5 per cent of the labour force. Creation of Employment based on Planning Commission's estimates.

The Planning Commission estimated for the most current year, i.e., up to March 1995. Indicating the unemployment rate that has increased from 4.29 per cent in 1991 to 5.51 in March 1995. The estimated values are based on current weekly status. Creating employment opportunities to absorb the existing unemployed and under - employed as well as the increase in labour force has been among one of the important concerns associating the policy of India. In discrimination measures to protect positive issues like three important components indicating credit marketing and technical help to encourage traditional and labour industry, incentive industry, there has formed the condition from the beginning to contine featured and implementation of policy inheriting throughout the past four decades. This concluded that the Industrial sector has been found robust throughout the period of growth and severe slow - down. The industrial performance of the 1990s took an initiation of fertile ground to investigate the performance of the various industries classified into three distinct parts.

1. The period immediately preceding the initiation of reforms - 1989 - 90 to 1992-93 making an indication of "crisis" period of 1990-91.
2. The period of rapid growth: 1993-94 to 1995-96.
3. The period of slow-down: 1996-97 to 1998-99.

In making performance of Indian industrial sectors, the employment programmes to the people of the country have undergone modifications and expansions. The continued expanded programmes specifying 'employment' have been stepped up substantially in successive five-year plans that suggested employment generation .In dealing successive plans, the important objective was accounted to create employment opportunities through labour intensive programme that could make identification of industrial growth during three stated above periods.

Employment Market Information (EMI) Programme in India

The EMI is mainly concerned with the Directorate general of Employment and Training (D.G.E & T), Ministry of labour, Government of India, and pertains to the year ended 31st March, 1996. This programme covers all organised establishments of the Public Sector, irrespective of their size and non-agricultural establishments in the private sector employing two or more persons.

Establishment in the Organised Sector

There were 2.75 lakhs establishments on the Employer's Register of Employment Exchanges at the end of March 1996 of these 1,62 lakh were in the public sector and the remaining 1.13 lakh in the private sector. In this connection, there was found declined tendency in the number of establishment both in the public and private sectors. The public sector establishment decreased from 1.64 lakh at the end of Mach, 1996 recording 1.62 lakh at the end of March, 1996 recording a decrease of 1.2 per cent . Further the employment in the organised sector went down from 279.87 lakh in Mach, 1995 to 277.80 lakh in March, 1996 indicating a decrease of 0.7 per cent. However, during the preceding year (1994-95) there was growth of the order of 2.2 that showed all zone/regions except North and South zone of the country such as:

Northern zone	:	6.0 per cent are increase in employment contributing highest.
Southern zone	:	2.7 per cent
Western zone	:	4.2 per cent
Eastern zone	:	2.6 per cent
Central zone	:	0.5 per cent

Following figures for the same period 1995 - 1996 provide a decrease in employment in classified industries of the country as mentioned below:

Wholesale and Retail Trade and Restaurants. And Hotels	:	0.9 per cent
Manufacturing	:	0.6 per cent
Mining and Quarrying	:	3.4 per cent
Electricity, Gas and Water	:	2.1 per cent

Construction	:	1.0 per cent
Community Social and Personal Services	:	0.8 per cent

Studying figures based on 1995 - 96, the numbers of educated job-seekers (Matriculates and above) increase from 239.97 lakh as at the end of December 1994 to 247.95 lakh as at the end of December 1995.

In this regard, an estimate has been made that a fall in the number of vacancies notified to the registration affected to the employment exchanges by various employers over the last ten years from 1986 being 11.3 per cent to 6.6 per cent in 1995 that appeared an alarming feature indicated as dispopularity of service in placement activities, which, being 6.3 per cent in 1986 came down to 3.7 per cent in 1996.

Employment in Industries/Services

The study provides a broad picture concerned with employment opportunities that have been expanded indirectly through increased income generation in India linked with effective capital-intensive production that created, new job to the employment since 31st March 1995 - 96 in the organized sectors under primary, secondary and tertiary. The figures for mentioned periods connected with employment opportunities in percentage distribution as mentioned below:

Table 1.11

Employment In Industries/Services by Categorized Industries/Services

Description of Industries/ services	*Employment (in lakh) As on 31st March 1995*	*1996*	*Percentage Change 1996/1995*	*2001 Projected*	*2002*	*02/01*
Primary sector	25.56	26.38	1.03	31.25	32.45	1.03
Agriculture, Hunting, Forestry and Fishing	14.39	15.59	1.08	21.16	23.14	1.09
Mining and Quarrying	11.17	10.79	0.06	8.65	7.92	0.91

Secondary Sector	76.28	76.43	1.00	77.20	77.96	1.00
Manufacturing	66.21	66.58	1.00	67.29	67.72	1.00
Electricity, Gas and Water	10.07	9.85	0.978	7.18	7.03	0.97
Constructions	12.18	12.06	0.99	11.94	11.85	0.99
Tertiary Sector	165.84	162.93	0.98	158.17	158.01	0.99
Wholesale and Retail Trade	4.76	4.81	1.01	5.40	5.32	0.98
Transport, storage and communication	31.57	29.96	0.94	22.18	21.92	0.99
Financing, Insurance, Real estate and Business Services	16.56	16.15	0.97	14.04	13.98	0.99
Community, Social and Personal Services	112.95	112.01	0.99	105.18	105.01	0.99
Total						

Source: Employment Review, 1995-96, Government of India, Ministry of Labour, Directorate of General of Employment and Training, New Delhi, 1999, p. 31.

Following interpretations might be inferred from above table as,

(i) The primary sector comprising agriculture, Hunting, Forestry and Fishing and Mining and Quarrying Industry divisions showed an over-all increase of only 3.2 % in the employment. Under this sector Agriculture, Hunting, Foresting and Fishing recorded growth of 8.4, where as the Mining and Quarrying divisions recorded a decrease of 3.4 per cent.

(ii) The growth in employment in the secondary sector was 0.2 %. Under this sector, employment in Manufacturing Division showed an increase of 0.6 % while employment in Electricity, Gas and Water Division and Construction Industry showed a decline of 2.1 % and 1.0 % respectively.

(iii) There was an overall decrease in employment in the tertiary sector of 1.8 %. The growth in employment in this sector was recorded only in Industry division. Wholesale and Retail Trade & Restaurant and Hotels (0.9 %) while all the other industry divisions recorded a fall in employment.

In conclusion, the increased and decreased trend of employment opportunities in different types of industry of the country may be explained as that the amount of indirect employment generation has been significantly reduced in many industries by high level of traditional job displacement caused by competition from modern manufacturing.

It is therefore clear that neither indirect effects of modern manufacturing nor any other by itself can resolve India's employment problem. There is thus a major role for the region's industry to play in providing work opportunities to the jobless.

Propositions for declining trend in employment opportunities.

This theory consists of four propositions.

- Traditional industry declined in India.
- It declined because of technological obsolescence, that is, it declined because hand-tools began to compete with machinery and lost.
- It is implied that this battle, which occurred in the market place, was forced by Britain's commitment free trade as an engine of growth.
- Closer economic relationship with Britain did create some modern industries in India such as textile mills, but the creative role of globalization did not approach in compensation of such destructive role.

In detail, a justification may be laid that Pre British rural India consisted of self sustaining egalitarian, village communities, producing their own subsistence. During the period, the British role, by its revenue policy, forced production for the market and, thus, broke up these communities.

Hence, it is therefore, the long-distance trade and regional markets untargeted on an unprecedented scale due to mainly, three factors, viz ; foreign trade, modern transport and communication, and the definition of contract law and private property affecting in dramatic manner an India's industry for which employment opportunities in different industries of the country could not create or extend in market labour and capital. Thus the association between falls in employment and technological obsolescence is rather weak, that is, there were several sectors where employment fell but no significant happened.

Existence of Employment Opportunities in Organised Manufacturing Sectors of India during 1980s - 1990s

It is obvious that employment opportunities in the organised manufacturing sector in India remained virtually stagnant in the 1980s. But in sharp contrast, there has been a substantial increase in employment in this sector in 1990s.

Evaluating statistical data based on organised manufacturing sectors, the growth rate of employment in the sectors was only 0.53 percent per annum between 1980-81 and 1990-91. But in the next five years, 1990-91 to 1995-96 the growth rate was much higher at 4.03 per cent per annum, comparing favourably with the growth achieved in the 1970s (about 3.8 percent per annum between 1970-71 and 1980-81). In the period 1990-91 to 1997-98 (the last year for which data are available), the growth rate of employment in organised manufacturing was 2.69 percent per annum, well above the growth rate achieved in the 1980s and higher than the growth rate of the labour force.

Reviewing the concept of growth rate of employment opportunities, the following table 2 provides the number of employment and growth rate in percent per annum since 1973-1978 in organised industry, private and public sectors. This study needed to stress on obtained results of growth rate of employment for such long period accounted for increased and decreased trend of employment opportunities in three industrial sectors.

Table 1.12

Growth in Employment in Organised Industry, Private and Public Sectors.

	Employment (000)				*Growth Rate (Percent per annum)*			
	1973-74	*1980-81*	*1990-91*	*1997-98*	*1973-80*	*1980-90*	*1990-97*	*2001-02 (projected)*
Public Sector	1365	2049	2323	2388	5.971	1.265	0.391	0.761
Private and Joint								

Sector (Including Unspecified)	4455	5666	5839	7658	3.495	0.302	3.715	3.319
Aggregate ASI (Including Electricity)	5820	7715	8163	9926	4.108	0.566	2.834	2.815

Source: ASI, CSO, Deptt. of statistics and Programme Implementation, Ministry of Planning and Programme Implementation.

The figures indicated in the above table 1.12 provided three period: 1973–2000, each of these periods a clear picture of growth rate of employment opportunity to the people of the country in organized industry (private and public sectors).

In observation, there grew employment rapidly. There was a sharp declination in employment growth in the 1980s in both public and private sector factories. In the 1990s, the growth rate of employment in public sector factories has come down further. It was only 0.4 percent per annum between 1990 - 91 and 1997 -98 by contest, the growth rate of employment in private sector factories has recovered and surpassed the growth rate prevailing in the 1970s with consequence that almost the entire increase in employment organised manufacturing that has taken place in the 1990s is accounted for by private sector factories.

Growth Rate of Employment Size Since 1973 - 1998

This study gives reflection on absorption of employment in organised sector (public and private sectors) emphasizing size structure (0-49, 50-99, 100-199, 200-499, 500 999, 1000-1999, 2000-4999, and 5000+) of factory. The purpose of the study was to distribution of employment (percent) as well as growth rate of employment (percent per annum).

Keeping in view of size structure of different factories of the country, the following table 1.13 distribution of employment accorded to factory size.

From the figures placed in above table 1.3 there resulted a marked change in the size structure in the 1980's and more so in the 1990's. The size class 50 to 500 employment gained while the size classes 2000 to 4999 and 5000 + lost heavily. In specified size structure 5000+ showed the most capital intensive (least labour-intensive)

Table 1.13
Distribution of Employment by Factory Size

Size Structure	Distribution of Employment (Percent)				Growth Rate (percent per annum)			
	1973-74	1980-81	1990-91	1997-98	1973-80	1980-90	1990-97	2001-02 (projected)
0-49	14.4	13.8	17.5	16.8	3.477	2.983	2.201	2.249
50-99	8.2	9.0	10.8	13.1	5.502	2.416	5.686	5.732
100-199	9.4	9.2	10.7	12.9	3.789	2.096	5.652	5.732
200-499	13.1	12.1	13.5	19.0	2.934	1.673	7.979	7.986
500-999	11.6	9.7	12.0	13.6	1.481	2.729	4.711	4.719
1000-1999	12.8	13.7	10.1	9.4	5.124	-2.454	1.815	1.913
2000-4999	16.7	15.9	9.5	10.0	3.381	-4.482	3.649	3.762
5000+	13.8	16.6	15.9	5.2	6.892	0.134	-12.436	-12.351
Total	100.0	100.0	100.0	100.0	4.108	0.566	2.835	2.843

Source :Same as table 2.

Also there was found sharp decline in the relative share of this size class in the 1990s and the increase in the relative shares of size classes 50-99, 100-199 and 200-499 must have made a significant contribution to employment growth in this period.

Employment Opportunity in Classified Industries of India

This study would give stress on classified industries. Key industries, transport sector, banking and other financial institution, and service sector. This is useful as a background for the subsequent presentation of data based on the reason for the acceleration in employment growth since 1995.

(a) Employment in Key industries:

To make concentration on four sub-industries comprising coal, cement, iron and steel and generation and transmission, the following table 1.14 has been used for assessing employment opportunities during 1995-96 so that percentage change might be evaluated for knowing full - employment strategy.

Table - 1.14

Industry Percentage Industries / Services change	Employment (in thous) As on 31st March					
	1995	1996	1996/95	2001	2002	02/01
1. Mining and agglomeration of coal	815.5	796.9	-2.3	750.4	734.3	0.97
2. Manufacturing of cement, lime and plaster	103.8	98.8	-4.8	85.5	80.01	0.93
3. Manufacturing of iron and steel in primary Semifinished forms	384.7	376.0	-2.3	365.2	352.5	0.96
4. Generation and transmission of electric energy	179.8	192.0	1.07	210.2	225.4	1.07

Source : Employment review, 1995 -96, Govt. of India, ministry of Labour, p. 35.

The analysed data of table 1.14 showed that employment in generation and transmission of electric energy had increased by 6.8 % while the other three key industries there was a decrease in employment of the country. The maximum decrease in employment was recorded in manufacturing of cement, lime, & plaster (4.8%), followed by meaning and agglomeration of coal and manufacture of iron and steel in primary and semi finished forms 2.3 per cent each. The decrease in different key industries require marked acceleration in employment growth as a result of economic reforms. There is some basis for taking such a view because, in certain ways, economic reforms are expected to have a favorable effect on the growth of employment in industries. The favorable effects may arise from greater labour market flexibility and increase trade orientation leading to changes in industrial scenario in favour of labour intensive industries and techniques of production as mentioned by Singh (1993) and Papola (1994).

Employment in Transport Sector

This is well know fact that transport industries is an important constituent of employment in the organised sector of the country consisting of five sub industries (table 15). In this regard, the distribution of employment is needed to find out percentage change for assumed years 1995 and 1996.

Table - 1.15
Employment in Transport Sector

Industry services	*Employment (in lakh) As on 31st March 1995*	*1996*	*Percentage Change 1996/1995*	*2001*	*2002*	*Percentage 02/01*
Railway transport	1339.9	1144.2	0.85	4168.7	3962.4	0.95
Passenger transport by bus, (Including Transways)	736.5	738.7	1.00	780.6	777.3	0.99
Ocean and coastal water transport	11.9	10.8	0.90	8.5	8.2	0.96
Inland water transport	29.8	29.4	0.98	27.3	26.9	1.08
Air transport carriers (of passenger and freight)	42.8	43.7	1.02	45.6	46.3	1.01

Source: Same as Table 1.4.

The employment rate of growth was found in decrease trend to all above sub-industries except for the case of Air transport carriers.

Further, the analysed data concerned with employment trends in banking and financial institution have been made under frame of four sub-industries to make extended concentration on explanation for acceleration in employment. In this context, the table 1.16 followed data based on employment banking industry and other financial institution for two assumed years 1995 and 1996.

Table 1.16
Employment in Banking Industry and Other Financial Institution

Industry services	*Employment (in lakh) As on 31st March 1995*	*1996*	*Percentage Change 1996/1995*	*2001*	*2002*	*Percentage 02/01*
Deposit Activities (Banking)	1185.9	1137.4	0.95	286.4	266.7	1.07
Other credit activities	84.7	84.8	1.00	3722.7	3712.7	1.0

Insurance carriers, life	128.2	123.8	0.96	275.4	276.2	0.99
Insurance carriers other than life	74.9	69.7	0.95	986.8	974.8	1.01

Source : Same as Table 1.14 and 1.15.

Table - 1.17
Employment In Service Sector

Industry services	*Employment (in lakh) As on 31st March 1995*	*1996*	*Percentage Change 1996/1995*	*2001 Projected*	*2002*	*Percentage 02/01*
Educational services rendered by Technical or vocational colleges, schools and other institutions	362.7	346.0	0.95	286.4	266.7	1.07
Educational services rendered by Non-technical colleges, schools etc	3772.7	3762.1	0.99	3722.7	3712.7	1.0
Research and scientific services	281.9	280.9	0.99	275.4	276.2	0.99
Health and Medical Services	1076.8	1049.5	0.97	986.8	974.8	1.01

Source : Same as table 1.4, 1.5 and 1.6.

There followed a gain in employment (2.5%) in Health and Medical services while other remained institutions rendered decreased trend in employment to the people of the country.

In estimating the key sector for economic growth, there can be assessed that expansion of manufacturing production also creates greater employment opportunities in the service sector. In this connection, the following table 1.18 provides three factors, viz.; 'Industry', 'Transport', and 'Energy' have been considered for direct contribution assessed manufacturing sectors that tend to generate the effective demand leading to employment expansion in our country :

Table – 1.18
Industry

Units	% change	1992-93	1993-94	1994-95	1995-96	1996-97	1997-98	1998-99	1999-00	2000-01
Index of Industrial Production	% change			8.9	13.1	6.1	6.6	3.8	8.1	7.5
Mining & Quarying	% Change			7.6	9.5	-1.9	5.9	-1.8	0.7	
Electricity	% Change			8.5	8.1	4.0	6.6	6.4	6.6	4.0
Manufacturing	% Change			9.1	14.1	7.3	6.6	4.1	9.1	8.8
Spun Yarn	% Change	7.5	10.4	2.7	13.0	12.4	6.4	-5.6	8.5	
Cement	% Change	1.0	6.7	7.9	11.5	9.6	9.1	5.6	14.1	
Fertilizers	% Change	-1.1	-6.6	15.3	8.2	-1.7	17.9	3.7	4.6	
Finished										
Steel	% Change	6.2	-0.2	17.0	20.3	6.1	0.8	3.2	10.1	
Automobile	% Change	-6.2	18.9	29.8	27.2	15.6	-4.4	-1.2	12.0	
Basic good	% Change			8.9	10.7	3.0	6.5	1.5	5.2	
Capital good	% Change			9.2	5.4	11.4	5.8	11.5	5.1	
Consumer good	% Change			12.1	12.8	6.2	5.5	1.9	5.4	

Intermediate Good	% Change			5.3	19.3	8.1	8.0	5.9	15.4	
Value of Out Put	Rs. Blm	3478	3922	4815	5896					
Gross value Added (Factor Sector)	Rs. Blm	689	812	1017	1261	4135				
Gross value Added (non-Factor Sector)	Rs. Blm	422	464	580	723	792				

Transport

Railways Freight Traffic	Mln. Tns	350.1	358.7	365.0	390.7	409.0	429.4	420.9	456.3	417.0
Cargo handled At major port	Mln. Tns	166.6	179.3	197.3	215.3	227.3	251.5	251.7	271.9	

Energy

Commercial Energy Products	% change	0.4	2.4	6.8	7.4	3.0	4.6	-0.5	1.1	
Commercial Energy Availability	% change	4.6	3.1	6.7	9.4	5.0	5.1	1.6	4.9	
Coal production (excl lignite)	Mln. tns	242.0	248.7	257.8	273.4	289.3	300.4	296.5	304.5	
Coal Imports	Mln. tns	6.1	6.8	10.1	11.9	12.7	15.9	14.8	19.3	
Power Capacity	Mw	72330	76753	81171	832294	85795	89167	93249	96682	
Electricity Generation (Pub. Ut.)	Bln. kwh	301.4	324.0	350.5	379.9	395.9	421.3	448.7	479.6	500.0
Thermal & Nuclear	Bln. Kwh	231.5	253.6	267.7	307.3	3235.9	346.8	365.3	399.0	

Hydel	Bln. Kwh	69.9	60.5	82.7	72.6	68.9	74.6	82.6	82.7	
T & D Losses	Percent	21.8	21.4	21.1	22.3	24.5				
Crude oil Production	Min. tns	27.0	27.0	32.2	35.2	32.9	33.7	32.7	32.0	32.0
Crude oil Import	Min. tns	29.2	30.8	27.3	27.3	33.9	34.5	39.8	57.9	68.0
Petroleum Products Imports	Min. tns	11.3	12.1	15.8	22.5	22.2	24.0	18.8	22.0	12.0
Consumption Of Petro Products	Min. tns	61.7	63.6	70.5	77.9	82.7	87.8	93.1	99.4	105.0
Consumption Of Petro Products	% change	3.4	3.2	10.8	10.5	6.1	6.3	6.0	7.9	6.0
Natural Gas gross Production	Bln. Cu. Mtrs.	18.1	18.3	19.4	22.6	23.2	26.4	27.4	28.0	
Natural Gas net Production	Bln. Cu. Mtrs.	16.1	16.3	17.3	21.2	21.5	24.5	25.7	26.3	

Source : CMIE (Centre for Monitoring Indian Economy), Monthly Review of the Indian Economy, Sept. 2000, pp. 4-5.

To analyse data in table 1.16 showed decrease trend in all stated industries except in the case of sub-industry, other credit activities. The figures presented for stated organised sector seemed disproportionate to the employment opportunities to the people of the country.

In the same way, an analysis concerned with education services, research and scientific services and health and medical that provided employment data for assumed years 1995 and 1996 as shown in the table 1.17.

The figures presented in above-mentioned table showed continuous process industries of various products in our country, which absorb labour utilization in both central manufacturing process and ancillary process resulting in greater employment generation in plant operation, as well as in distribution. This study revealed that industrial employment expansion in India followed greater and extended form of job opportunities in processing various industries located at different areas among the masses.

Some Analytical Considerations

India's manufacturing industries classified in (i) Registered (Organised), and (ii) Unregistered (Unorganised) sectors. The former sector employed about 10 percent of the workforce to produce about 16 percent of measured GDP, while the latter sector accounted for bulk of the workforce. Though in the initial years of planning much of the development strategy focused on creating a large and efficient capital goods industries. In this connection, Lucas (1989) and Datt Chaudhri (1995) remarked about poor performance in policy-induced rigidities and industrial labour market that practically stopped employment growth in the country from a different analytical perspectives, rate of employment growth that can be expanded due to adaption of following reasons;

(a) Starting from wage reduction to employee for increasing employment opportunities in different industry;
(b) Real holding of healthy output growth;
(c) Having greater attention towards labour market to be the 'active' market with the product market following the labour market;
(d) Enforcing induced policy for adoption of large such and ever increasing installation of industries to the urban areas in search of more viable employment opportunities.

(e) Bringing a fundamental change in inducing full employment programme by means of increased output, effective and justified distribution of income, and stimulated consumer demand in most acceptable and effective processes ;

(f) Implicating equally important "modern" technologies, with the scale of operations and political and economic linkages for not displacing labour absorbing of small, indigenous enterprises and small scale agriculture.

(g) Establishing the seriousness of the employment problem and having need to redirect current strategies of development ;

(h) Examining the labour absorbing potential in the various economic sectors following importance of directly generating additional employment emphasising modern manufacturing

(i) Indicating various ways of application of appropriate and proportionate technologies in favour of responded employment opportunities to maximise contribution in employment generation.

References

1. Sec NSSO (1996).
2. Sec Planning Commission (1999).
3. Classification of persons working or employed according to different methods.
4. Sec Sidhu (1991) for a brief review of the literature on the subject and also for further evidence in support of the view.
5. Presidential Address to the Indian Society of Labour Economics in 1997 at Tirupati, see Lakdawala (1993).
6. See Hashim (1998).
7. Hashim, S.R. (1998),"Economic Growth ad Income Distributin – The Indian Experience of Development". Economic & Political Weekly, Vol.33, No.12 March 2.
8. Lakdawla, D.T. (1993), :"Growth, Unemployment and Poverty", in Papola, T., S., P, P. Ghosh and Alakh N. Shharma (eds.), Labour, Employment & Industrial Relations in India, B.R., Publishing Corporation for the Indian Society of Labour Economics, Delhi.
9. Planning Commission (1992), Ninth Five Year Plan, 1997-2002, Vol. 1, Development, Goals, Strategy and Policies, Govt. of India, New Delhi.
10. NSSO (1996), Employment and Unemployment in India 1993-1994, Fifth Quinquennial Survey, NSS Fifth Round (July 1993-June 1994),

National Sample Survey Organisation, Department of Statistics, Government of India, New Delhi.

11. Sidhu, H.S. (1991), "Unemployment Poverty Nexus : Another Look", The Indian Journal of Labour Economics, Vol. 34, No. 2.

2

Growth Rate of Employment in Indian Industrial Sectors

The growth rate of employment in Indian Industrial sectors approaches the consideration of employment data based on assumption to the change in the size structure in favour of small and medium industries and slow down in the growth in real wages.

The economic analysis to derive the guidelines of a policy needed to maximise employment and to bring about an improvement in the standard of living of the workers. For this purpose, the present chapter is to use a system, comprising four 'sub-systems', that defines the relations between employment, wages, productivity, profits, prices and money in terms of equations given at the end. The 'system' disregard, as distinct from guidance and exploitation, of the market forces. The more the institutional base of an economy makes it exogenously determined, the more does it become internally weak, contradictory and inhibitive.

The underlying assumptions of the system', though of general applicability, make it particularly valid for the development phase of a developing economy. These are;

(i) Labour and capital are the only sources of income. All workers whether employees, independent workers or employers often derive their income from both those sources. Income earned by the application of labour is wages and that by capital is profit. Rent and interest are only special categories of profit or income from capital. Employees receive their income from component of the income of independent workers is included in prices of their product. In consequence, agricultural prices have the same significance for workers in agricultural industry as money wage rates for employees. In brief, due to the predominance of peasant farming and household industry, there is little class stratification while functional factor and producer prices are not always distinct categories

(ii) No one fails to see the ' price-tag', even when a part of the produce is meant for direct consumption by the producers. There is no money- illusion. On the contrary, if prices increase, employees insist on a compensatory increase in money wages, the independent workers on higher prices of their products and the capitalists on higher returns. There may be a 'concealment' but there is no hoarding of money.

(iii) In the event of wage-price flexibility the market will clear itself at full employment. Money wages are, however, rigid and downwards while institutional arrangements keeping them above marginal productivity value in case of harbour unemployment. Administered prices lead to similar disequilibria in both factor and product markets.

(iv) At low levels of income there is little difference between the consumption standards of the employed and the unemployed. It, therefore, follows, that at the macro level total consumption corresponds to total wage income and savings equal only profit income.

(v) Liquid assets in the form of money of bullion may be concealed to evade taxation or law. Concealed money, however, is not hoarded. It circulates in an illegitimate market to which it withdraws resources from production and legitimate distribution.

Given these parameters, the volume and incidence of unemployment is caused by the wage-up i.e. by the difference between wage and the value of marginal product of available labour. Labour supply is a function of the money wage rate and the entire labour force available at the current wage. Beyond this, labour supply may still increase with a rise in money wages though at a less than proportionate rate as fresh supplies are to be drawn by raising the labour force participation rate. Demand for labour, on the other hand, depends upon the comparative value of marginal product of labour and the money wage. Given perfect wage-flexibility, equilibrium would be established at full employment and wage would equal marginal product value. But due to the downward inflexibility of the current wage, a wage-gap would leave workers, with marginal productivity lower than the current wage, unemployed. There is a 'real employment-gap' corresponding to the 'wage-gap'. Actual unemployment may, however, be less then this as the institutional factors may compel several plants and industries to give employment even to surplus hands whose marginal product is lower or zero. Total employment is limited by real wage-fund i.e. the product of the labour force and its marginal output. Hence an increase in money wages without an increase in marginal productivity of labour reduces directly the volume of employment. Alternatively, employment of surplus workers affects adversely the earnings of workers actually needed to do the job.

Money-wage and wage-differentials are primarily historical, fixed at subsistence level(s). Any correspondence of the historical money wages with labour productivity value is only incidental. Another component is added to the historical wage to compensate directly or indirectly for the rise in prices and cost of living. So long as prices continue to increase, wage claims for upward revisions cannot be wholly denied. A third component of the money-wage is determined by the rate of profit whose changes measure the gains in labour productivity as well as the capacity and costs of admitting or denying larger wage claims. It is, however, not necessary that this component may invariably take the form of a profit bonus as it may equally enter a general bonus, higher wage rate, periphery benefits or extended welfare programmes. In this wage-profit relation, and irrespective of its form, there is a built-in inflationary potential which both labour and management often agree to reinforce. Finally, a part of the money wage is the result of the institutional base of the market. This consists of customary practices, incentive or other payments and prices system, statutory regulations of wages and prices including fixation of minimum or fair wages, legal prescription of labour-management relations, mobility of labour, trade unionism, collective bargaining, system of land tenures with reference to the agriculturists, and the like. All these contribute an institution induced component to wages.

Real wage depends on the amount of the money wage and prices governing the cost of living. It is, however, not necessary that money and real wages may move together. For instance, when money wages increase without a corresponding increase in labour productivity, prices and cost of living invariably rise. This may often more than neutralise the rise in money wage and thus the real wage may actually fall. An improvement in the standard of living of the workers or real wage, can be attained only through increased labour productivity.

Labour productivity in the 'system' is found to be a function of the stock of capital-in-use in comparison to the labour force or simply the capital-labour ratio, the relative factor prices i.e. wages in relation to the cost of capital goods that determine the level of technology and the institutional base governing the production relations and incentives. Capital in-use as the balance of the accumulated stock of capital and capital lying idle, is related to the total investments upto the end of the preceding period, the level of output corresponding to the aggregate outlay and the composition of capital at the time in comparison to the basket of goods that is demanded. Idle capacity thus results from a low level of investments (consumption function being constant) and the difference in the pattern of demand in relations to what can be produced. This latter may arise on account of a strategy of unbalanced growth, changes in development priorities or excess demand created suddenly by whether failures in agriculture or mounting international tensions and wars. Investment at any time is limited on the supply side not only by the availability of domestic savings and foreign capital but equally by the financial structure, that governs the mobilisation of available investment resources. In this lies the crucial role of the financial intermediaries — banking and non-banking alike—in helping or hindering the mobilization of transferable savings and resources into priority production channels. Besides the role of financial intermediaries, the entire process of the creation of credit and supply of money including foreign exchange and the holding of gold and silver is significant in determining the money flows and the supply of transferable savings. Total investment, however, is not determined simply by supply conditions. The demand for investment plays a significant role as the supply of resources. There is nothing like the supply of investible resources creating their own demand. Investment demand is determined by (i) availability of credit, not in the aggregate but to the individual producer, industry or sector on the security that it can offer; (ii) the wage-gap governing the return margin on capital rather than the rate of interest whose changes make little differences in costs; (iii) the current rate of growth of the economy determining expectations; and (iv) the market-barriers to new investment. This task is a complex of market imperfection, restrictive trade practices, inadequacy of enterprise and statutory limitations on it, excessive rates of taxation, demarcation of boundaries of flows of factors and products, and cumbersome and dilatory administrative procedures for incorporation, acquisition of land, licenses for production or sales and purchases of domestic or foreign goods, etc. Domestic savings, that primarily limit real resources available for investment, are given by the difference between the total output and the product of the volume of employment and the money wage. Total consumption is determined by the latter and, therefore, excess employment and higher money wage both reduce saving. There is, therefore, no escape from wage restrains for maximizing savings necessary for enlarging output and employment as well as for raising real wages.

The 'sub-system' of money, profits and prices reveals that the volume of money multiplied by its income velocity must equal the total of wage and profit incomes. Money supply can seldom be limited when wage and profit incomes are rising. Any monetary controls under these conditions are rendered weak by income induce changes in income velocity of money. Further, since there is no money illusion, additions to money supply soon raise money wages and profits. The profit rate is strangely interlocked with the money wage rate and the ratio of concealed liquid assets to total money supply. In so far as the latter offers opportunities of higher returns on capital in unlawful trades like smuggling, black marketing, hoarding and illegitimate speculation, the returns on capital increase directly with the proportion of concealed liquid assets. Finally, the total output on the supply side is limited by the complex of market structure determining factor availability and their allocation. This complex is given by the institutional base, market barriers, financial structure, availability of credit and the ration of concealed liquid assets to total money supply. The aggregate demand for total goods and services equals the sum of the total money wages and profits. Consequently, with a rise in wages and profits without a corresponding increase in aggregate output, prices inevitably rise as a balancing items. In our 'system', neither supply creates its own demand nor does demand create its own supply. The system has neither a perfect Sayian nor Keynesian solution. Its stability conditions have to be derived from a recognition of supply limitations on the one hand and wages and profits induced inflationary demand potential on the other.

In essence, the market complex determines employment, output and growth in the 'system'. An 'inferior' market complex distorts market structure and weakens most of the economic discipline inherent in competition for productivity gains. A 'superior' market complex, on the other hand, leads to optimum output, employment and wages. Looked at from another angle, variations in money wages play a crucial role in the 'system'. But these variations are not independent of the institutional base and of profit and price movements originating in finance. No direct wage-price policy can keep money wages on an even keel. A proper approach lives through the introduction of a 'superior' market complex.

Alternative Estimates of Employment and their Time Trends:

All the unemployment rates and aggregates which can be calculated from data collected in 10 rounds of the National Sample Survey (Referred to as NSS thereafter) between 1978-79 and 1997-98 and the Censuses of 1981 and 1991 are summarised in for referred studies two crucial distinctions are required for the interpretation of these data : (a) between time-rates and person-rates of unemployment and (b) between "current status" and "usual status" rates of unemployment.

(a) The first distinction arises from the fact that the unemployment rate may be measured either in units or labour time or in numbers of unemployed persons. The time-rate is the number of person-days of unemployment as a proportion of person-days of labour supply per week. The person-rate is calculated with the number of persons counted as unemployed on the basis of their status during a preceding reference period. This number is divided by the number of persons in the labour force in the same period.

The time-rate and the person-rate may also be regarded as the flow rate and the stock rate of unemployment respectively.

(b) The second distinction refers to the fact that some unemployment rates are measured on the basis of employment status over a short reference period, usually a week preceding the census/survey, and others on the basis of employment status over a long reference period, usually a year preceding the census/survey. They are called current status rates and usual status rates, respectively.

An interesting feature of the most recent 27th and 32nd Round NSS data for 1772-73 and 1977-78 is that they yield three different unemployment rates :[4] the "usual status" rate, and two "current status" rates, the "weekly status" rate and the "daily status" rate. The usual status and weekly status rate are person-rates (or stock-rates). The daily status rate is a time-rate (or flow-rate).

The daily status unemployment rate is the ratio of labour days per week reported as unemployed (seeking or available for work) to the total labour force days per week (working plus seeking plus available days). Thus if a person wanted work for 6 days in the reference week and could get it for 5 days only, his / her daily status unemployment rate would be 16.6 percent. The aggregate daily status rate for a week will then be a sighted sum of the rates for individual sample workers.[5]

In contrast with daily status unemployment, weekly status unemployment is measured in number of persons. A person's status for the whole week, called the "current status". Is determined as follows: Every person who worked for gain for at least one hour on at least one day during the reference week, just preceding the survey, is given the "working" or "employed" status. Others are classified as "seeking" or "available" or "not available" for work. Thus anybody who worked for an hour in the week or was available for work would be in the labour force. And only those persons would be counted as unemployed ("seeking work" or "available" for work) who did not work for a single hour in the week and were in the "seeking" or "available" position for a part of the week. With these definition we should evidently expect the weekly status unemployment rate to be lower than the daily status rate.

The "usual status" unemployment rate is also a person-rate. At the time of the survey, a person is given a single status based on his "usual" status during the preceding year. All except those "usually" out of the lobour force in the previous year are counted as members of the force, and only those who were "usually" unemployed are counted as unemployed. Therefore the usual status rate should be expected to be the lowest of the three rates.

On the basis of above statement the present chapter is to analyse the generation of a high rate of growth of employment which follows as a joint product of certain general economic policies of efficient production to implement the aforementioned conflict resolution instead of being viewed in terms of adhoc schemes of employment creation as part of social-welfare programme, external to the production plan and in conflict with growth.

For the purpose of reaching the objective in the minimum time it has been shown to be optimum for a country. The Heavy Investment sector would be made to growth at the fasted possible, through the avoidance of leakage of its capacity towards the consumption good sector. The low actual priority to intergenerational equity has been the effect of a low rate of plough back of investment. This followed from the fact those huge amounts of products of Heavy Investment have been used for the benefit of the consumption sector, firstly for the manufacture of Mechanised Light Machiery (MLM), and secondly, for the provision of processed material, fuel and power from the H-sector sources for the production of consumption goods. The mechanised Light Machinery strategy which has been followed for the first five plans has not merely kept the rate growth of employment low in the consumption sector, but what is more important, it has decreased the rate of growth of the Heavy Investment sector, for it has diverted the physical product of that sector away from its own expansion. It has found the best form of production in large scale enterprises, and this has led to monopolism on the one side and metropolitanism on the other side.

Obviously, the planning policy followed by the government up to now, however since they may have been in their attempt to attain socialistic or welfare objectives, has in actuality neither achieved the best interest of the long run, nor attended in substantial measure to the requirements of short term social justice. It is the correct strategy, which has frustrated the achievement of the social objectives, and the responsibility of its falls upon the economic community in the first instance, rather than on the political or collective choice.

Impact on Employment due to Consequences of Economic Liberalisation

The consequence of economic liberation on employment has been served in a debate held in South Asia for Consideration of 'growth of labour force and total employment. For India as well as her four neighbouring countries Bangladesh, Pakistan, Sri Lanka and countries of South Asia. The debate has been held for two mentioned factors since 1975-1993 in terms of percent as given in table 2.1.

Table 2.1

Growth Of Labour Force, Total Employment

Countries	*Growth rate of labour force*				*Growth rates of total employment*				
	1975-80	*1981-85*	*1986-93*	*2000-2001*	*1975-80*	*1981-85*	*1986-93*	*2000-2001*	*2001-2002 (projected)*
Bangladesh	2.19	2.79	2.99	3.02	-	-	5.37	-	58.83
India	1.73	2.02	1.02	1.67	2.36	1.77	1.93	2.69	
Pakistan	2.97	3.24	2.66	2.72	3.32	2.07	1.93	1.72	
Sri Lanka	2.72	1.64	1.51	1.47	1.65	-4.84	12.08	12.67	
South Asia	1.91	2.18	205	2.35	-	-	-	-	

Note: Employment growth rates for India for National Sample Survey data on employment and unemployment for 1977 to 2002.

Source: ILO (2002).

The figures in above table 2.1 show that rate of growth of employment has not declined for India in 1990s while Sri Lanka showed very high growth in the 1990s. On the other hand, in Pakistan the trend of decline in the growth of employment continued even in the 1990s. The table also shows that the growth rate of labour force in South Asia over the past two decades has been around 2 percent.

In light of above study, the following table 2.2 shows growth rates of employment to the manufacturing industries (organised and unorganised) for India since 1973-1994.

Table 2.2

Manufacturing Employment Growth 1973-2001

	1973-78	1978-83	1983-88	1988-94	2000-2001
Total manufacturing	5.83	3.23	3.00	1.34	1.27
Organised manufacturing	4.88	1.86	-0.45	2.31	2.03
Unorganised manufacturing	6.16	3.69	3.97	1.08	1.09
Small-Scale Industrial Sector	7.99	7.90	6.26	4.51	4.21

Source : Goldar (2001).

The figures contained in table 2.2 provides an emperical evidences (1973-94) to the manufacturing sector of the country. They show a marked declaration in employment growth in the manufacturing sector as a whole over time. In the case of organised manufacturing, the growth rate declined significantly till 1988 but picked up during 1088-94. On the other hand, there has been a continuous decline in the rate of growth of employment in unorganised manufacturing and the SSI (Small Scale Industries) sector. The growth for there sectors during 1988-94 was lower than that of earlier periods. But it may be noted that the growth of employment in the small-scale sector is still higher than that in organized scale sector.

Further, the growth rate of employment as registered in case ot manufacturing industries for India for the period 1973-74 to 1995-96, 2000-2001 as presented in the following table 2.3.

Table 2.3

Distribution of Employment in Registered Manufacturing India 1973-2001

Year	Growth rate (percent)
1973-74 to 1979-80	1.4
1980-81 to 1988-89	-0.6
1973-74 to 1982-83	3.4
1986-87 to 1994-95	2.1
1986-87 to 1995-96	4.0
1998-99 to 2000-2001	4.93

Source: Nagraj (1994, 1999, 2001).

For registered manufacturing organised sectors of the country, the following conclusions can be drawn as:

1. The growth rate declined from 1.4 per cent during 1973-80 to –0.6 per cent during 1980-89.

2. The negative growth rate in the 1980s is found misleading as the figure shows there were only four years (1983-84 to 1987-88) when employment fell is absolute figures. After negative growth in the mid-eighties, employment showed a steady increase, and the absolute levels are higher in the 1990s.

3. For the period 1986-87 to 1995-96, where there is found post-liberalization, the employment growth was quite high in 1995-96 and associated with high industrial growth rate (13 percent) during that year.

4. Employment growth was not affected by negative growth in output during 1997-94. The employment growth reflects the rise in fixed capital formation after the reforms.

5. In aggregate level of employment rate, the liberalization programme (1991) did not show any adverse effect:

Concentration on employment and consumption disparities:

In fact, a factor which has a great bearing on employment policy in the rate of growth of consumption levels for the persons already in the organised sector. The increase of consumption standards may be observed to occur among the entrepreneurs, and executives in business as well as in other organizations or in government, and is oriented luxury and semi-luxury goods from the point of view of the mass of population. In consumption surveys, in terms of money, the disparities in standards of living between the strata of society purchasing these goods and the medium consumption level are somewhat under-estimated.

Further, in order to concentrate on given subject, the ingredients follow two aspects viz. employment policy indicating (i) the role of growth of consumption of person to any organised or unorganized sectors that standardized the situation of entrepreneurship, and the executiveness in business activities recognized for governmental or non-governmental organizations where level of standard is being stratified in various form for the use of capital investment, (ii) a fixed expenditure that makes an indication of consumption-expenditure as desired level of significance in terms of money. Such practices follow strategy for intergenerational equity depending upon consumption for rapid economic growth.

In addition to, the strategy for intergenerational equity requires restraint on the consumption of self employed population as well as that of privileged section of workers and salary earners. Such fundamental proportion of equalitarian thought follow the large volume of subscription to national-saving asset promoted in increased form of consumed goods with equitable distribution through larger employment consideration because the consumption sector concentrate upon production of necessary consumed goods brought for austerity and restraint in rise of standard of living in diverse form. Such thought is applied for organised sectors where real wages are being ascribed to privileged or unprivileged class in stratified section of the society but in differentiation a larger universe of people of the organized sector alien in the economy, the growth process has to be supplied with epithic of illegitimacy described in growth process.

To have broad thought in the sphere of organised modern industrialized and agriculture activities depending upon mass of humanity where multiple of persons engaged with the circle of organised employment, all are meant for bringing into productive fold of organised production with equitable growth process through long-term universe following in manner of persuasive and efficient rapid expansion in the universe. With however, changes in employment policy when undertaken into consideration should be the objective of employment policy to draw into the organised sector provides employment opportunities for large population in an indication of efficient production.

In this context, Lord Keyness was quite specific that relevance of investments for the welfare of those most needing the goods is paramount and came down heavily against employment created through pyramid building (or singing masses for the dead) or projects for focusing the dead when many of the living were homeless. Nor merely has it got to be, as professor Michael Kalecki has suggested (in consonance with Keynessian thinking) for investment to be in programmes of social welfare. The best programme of social welfare for providing employment to the working population outside the sphere of present employment is to invest in productive activities, which provide for the present and future in a balanced way.

The rapid expansion of productivity provides the techniques of high labour-productivity used in highly mechanised large scale industry for generating the impression of great employment generation where the scale and degree of mechanisation appropriate to the sectors to implement strategy for intergenerational equity and to cover techniques of production of consumption necessary at desired level of the strategy alien organised employment. In dealing with organised and unorganised workers the advocacy is being determined by measures of orientation and skill.

Besides, the above ingredients for creation of employment, there is intended to give remarks for welfare of the society to any geographical region subject to the conditions of accelerated production laid in dealing with economics of production and not of charity. For economy of production, there exist adequate funds with greater intensity that brings employment consideration to the regions.

In order to make assertion on employment conditions for welfare of the society, the determinental factors of employment are classified into non-employment, marginal employment, in inferior occupation, idleness, and in capacitated activities- all these categories occurs in the sphere of economy to any geographical region of the world and the conditions may be identified as 'proper' identification to proper assessment in the country particularly stressing on Bihar state which is also regarded for seasonal employment affecting both rural and urban sectors of the states. To both rural and urban sectors there is made 'labour adjustment' though it is more complex, because, the enterprises refrain from increased workforce with view to effect competitive compulsions: Accordingly, the enterprises opt either for more capital intensive technology or contract in increased volume of work to small enterprises where the provisions of government permission do not apply there.

Further neoclassical analysis where the rate of growth is found depending upon the rate of saving to any individual or mass of the population within organised economy, for economics to any developing nation unlike India, the noble laureate professor Sir Arthur Lewis formulated growth theory depending upon rate of growth rate on saving characterised by either increased or decreased trend for the Sen's of employment opportunities. The author remarked that the concept of full employment depending upon the rate of growth of population and of technical progress is induced to undertake a high quantum of capital investment without any decrease in real wage rate to paid workers weather the workers are assigned for high or low payment.

In the context of given subject, Dr. Moffat (one of the followers of Chalmars) introduced the concept of 'economy of consumption' in year 1878 stated about the idea of worker saving rather than entrepreneurial thrift by stating it is not function of the workers to provide capital for investment but of the entrepreneurs who are bound to invest capital for entrepreneurship (whether modern of socialist).

So far as, jobless growth concept has been brought due to reason of job security regulations introduced in the late 1970s and strengthened in the early 1980s in the organised manufacturing sector. He has also argued '*diperity* taxes' considering as one of the dictum, of direct taxation to any development oriented economy under the provision of non-differentiation rather to achieve resources of the economy from further production.

Empirically, result with view to economic theory under assumption of macro proposition concerned with employment situation prevailing in the country followed with theoretical as well as practical perspective in analysing data procurred from census of the country and NSSs (a governmental organisation). Such study has been presented on the following economy advocated in Indian economic associations annual conference at Madras (Dec. 1977). The analysis of procured data could be made under the following hypothesises. The framed hypothesises have been undertaken into consideration of aggregate supplies of wage goods, wage rate, wage-paid employment, government real expenditure, real National income, wage goods supplies and population, capital stock and output and capital ratio, and the proportion of government expenditure in real National income and the capital output ratio. For mentioned factors included in the study of Indian economic relevant to the dynamics of the employment situation. The researcher of the present study could frame the hypothesises under which different remarks might be given statistically. Besides, a comment had also been placed for estimated values obtained for the case of the population concerned with employment situation in both agricultural and industrial sectors.

Framed hypothesies:-

1. Wage paid unemployment is positive and significantly related to the aggregate supplies of wage-goods and negative and significantly related to the real wage rate.

2. When wage-paid employment is regressed over wage-goods supplies and the output of heavy industry, the former alone is statistically significant.

3. Government real investment expenditure has a more powerful statistically significant effect upon wage-paid employment than real government expenditure.

   There is no statistically significant relation between real wages and per capital real consumer expenditure, the latter as worked out from NSSs.

4. Money wages by themselves have positive effects upon wage-paid employment, since prices of consumption goods have been rising at higher rate than money wages. It follows that in the wage-paid sector, that is in the organised sector, there is some positive relation between inflation and employment, but this is a partial truth. In economy as a whole the burden of unemployment is passed on to the unorganised sector particularly in the rural areas.

5. When real national income is regressed over capital stock, population and land, population is seen not to have any statistically significant effect upon real income.

6. There is a highly statistically significant and positive relation between wage-goods supplies and population.
7. There is significant and negative relation between capital stock and output capital ratio. This is also in the wage-goods sector.
8. The rate of profit in the economy has a statistically significant inverse relation with the share of wages, the proportion of government expenditure in real national income, and the capital output ratio. Real national income is s statistically significantly accounted by capital stock and wage-goods supply, in relation to the above two factors, government real expenditure or real investment do not have a statistically significant effect upon real national income.

Following proportions may be undertaken into consideration of employment opportunity in manufacturing sectors;

(i) Given the macro capital-employability ratio, the larger the stock of capital the larger would be the volume of employment. This is provided that capital output ratio remains unchanged.

(ii) Given the stock of capital and its rate of growth the lower is the capital-employability ratio, the larger will be the volume of employment and the higher its rate of growth, provided the capital output ratio remains unchanged.

(iii) Given the capital stock and its rate of growth and the capital-employability ratio the lower is a capital output ratio the larger would be the employment and the higher its rate of growth.

(iv) If the population size is larger in relation to the stock of capital and if the rate of population growth is also relatively higher, the employment situation should not tend adversely. All this assumes that the composition of capital and of output would be appropriate to suit the requirements of the need following from employment.

Thus, we can broadly list the factors relevant to the dynamics of the employment situation:

(i) The size of population, its rate of growth, the change in age composition, and the change in the proportion of the labour-participant rate to population.

(ii) The stock of capital and its rate of growth, abstracting from problems of measurement of capital

(iii) The composition of capital and changes thereof particularly concerning the proportion of circulating capital to total capital, itself partly determined by the proportion to productive capacity of that devoted to product goods demand as circulating capital.

(iv) The level of the real wage rate, the level of the mean-consumption rate of the self-employed, the structure of wages and earnings and changes in all these factors;

(v) The information framework concerning availability of employment opportunities and terms there of, the condition of accessibility to the above information, transport and communication activities facilitating mobility conditions governing intra-regional and inter-regional mobility and change in all these factors;

(vi) Institutional conditions governing the maintenance of the unemployed and the level of consumption at which they are maintained.

These are the six sets of factors that enter into the determination of aggregate employment and its rate of change in a country.

Some statistical evidence are available related to above factors. Consideration of populations and labour force, around early fifties the rate of population growth based on the censuses of 1941 and of 1951 was placed at about 1.3% per annum. Around late seventies the population growth rate is estimated at between 2.3% and 2.6%. The Census of 1987 alone will tell us exact position. The linear rate (semi-logo) was 2.0% per annum between 1950-51 to 1962-63, this has risen to 2.20% for the period 1962-63 to 1975-76. These estimates are based on the population projections as given by the statistical authorities. According to the data given in the NSS Reports there seems to be a rising tendency in the average size of the house holds. This has steeply risen particularly among rural labour households, from 4.5 in 1963-64 to 4.70 in 1974-75 and among agricultural labour households from 4.47 to 7.74. The number of rural households too has risen from 70.4 million in 1964.65 to 82.1 million in 1974-75, an increase of 16.6 percent in a decade. It has not yet been possible for us to finally discern any noticeable reduction in the birth rates. However, medical and sanitation facilities have been continuously improving and the death rates seem to be on the downward trend. It would be safe to presume that the population of people falling in the age group 15-59. This is natural in a context in which death rates are falling. Particularly among the lower age groups the average expectation of life has risen, it is currently around 53 as compared to about thirty-three decades ago: people in general seem to be living longer. One should not wonder, therefore, that a rising proportion of people above 60 would be offering themselves for work in competition with those below 60. We should, therefore, find that a certain amount of proportion of the population competes for diversed jobs.

Further, the labour participation ratio among the population in the working group too should be rising. The NSS data is not helpful here because it excludes the category of labour concealed as helpers in cultivating households. In the non-agricultural sector too the proportion of such helpers should be high. As mentioned earlier, according to earlier census type data the labour participation ratio should be above 40 percent of the people belonging to the working age group. The NSS records a ratio of only about 30 per cent. There seems to be some concealment of labour participation. The bulk of labour not revealing itself as 'labour participants' in the NSS data should be demand to be disgustedly unemployed. According to the commerce and the NSS there is a steeply rising tendency in the proportion of agricultural labour to total populations. The bulk of them are landless labourers or own characterising fragmentation of land. In 1974-75, the average acres cultivated by agricultural labours household was 1.11 acres as contrasted with 1.15 acres for rural labour households. 60 per cent of the latters cultivated land less then half on acre. The incidence of weekly status unemployment as also the rate of underemployment is quite high among agricultural labour. One may hazard the hypothesis that the NSS observed unemployment and underemployment itself reflects an aspect of disguised underemployment.

There is no evidence of a backward-sloping supply curve of labour in India. On the other hand with rising prices and earnings not keeping pace with prices, the pressure to work is rising. This is particularly so among females. The very high incidence of larger daily status unemployment both in rural and urban areas and the high casualty rate among children in the high schools in some evidence of the pressure of need for supplementary earnings.

Capital stock in the economy has been growing since early fifties at a linear rate of 5 percent per annum 1950-51 to 1962-63, this rate was 4.50 per cent per annum. Prior to 1950-51 the capital stock was growing definitely at a lower rate, may be less than 2 per cent per annum. By itself the rising tendencies in the rate of growth of capital stock should be a maximum features but unfortunately in India we have been benefiting the phenomenon more or less of a continuously rising drift in the capital output ratio.

The average proportion of net output to capital which was around 42 to 43 per cent in early fifties came down to 38-40 per cent during the early sixties: this has further gone down to about 30 per cent around the close of the seventies. The incremental ratio has gone down from around 42 per cent to 20 per cent and less. The Draft plan for 1978-83 contemplated an incremental ratio of less than 20 per cent. The capital-out put ratio has risen in almost all sectors, in power, transport, housing, industry as well as agriculture. A number of reasons have been adduced for this rising trend: There has been a rise in the proportion of high capital out put ratio activities to low-capital output ratio activities. Secondly, the unit cost of an increment in power, transport, industry and agriculture has risen. Additional projects exploit costlier resources. For example, cheaper sites for hydro-electric generation and thermal plants were naturally exploited first. Similarly, in mining and also in manufacturing sites and in the construction of railways lines. Forest and timber resources are getting quickly eroded. Raw material supplies are getting more and more expensive for basic and heavy industries. Construction costs are going up because of the rising expenses of production in cement and construction materials. In agriculture too the best land had already been taken for cultivation. The growth of new area has been proceeding at less than 1 per cent since mid sixties. Further the growth of agricultural production has shown increased that depends upon inputs of organic chemicals, diesel oil, etc. There is no doubt at all that each new project involves more unit costs per unit output than earlier. The capital output ratio takes into account the impact of whatever technological changes that has already taken place and absorbed.

Development during the last three decades in India has seen a rise in the relative share of employment in the organised portions in manufacturing finance, transport and communications, government services, hotels, consultancy services, etc. Most of employment in these sectors occurs in urban areas. The rate of growth of employment in the organised sector in linear terms has ruled at about 3.70 per cent for the period 1950-51 to 1975-76. During 1950-51 to 1962-63 it was 2.80 per cent but during 1962-63 to 1975-76 this rate went up to 3.70 per cent. It is well known that the organised sectors has higher levels of wages and salaries then in the unorganised rural sector. Naturally out of the gross wages-fund a rise in the proportion of employment in the organised sector would imply a proportionately larger drift. As a result, what is available to the rest of economy shrinks in proportion. Since wages goods supplies have grown recently only at about 2 per cent per annum whereas the employment in the organised sector has risen at about 3.70 per cent per annum, it is quite possible that the absolute share of the wages-fund for the non-organised sector has even got reduced. This might be one of the reasons for the growth in rural distress which has been a conspicuous phenomenon in India in recent years. It is true that the real cost of living in urban areas is 20 to 25 per cent higher, yet since the mean wage rate here would be at least three-fourths above that in an unorganised sector, the redistribution effect on command over wage-goods in favour of the organised sector is obvious.

The information framework regarding employment has been expanding. Employment exchanges have increased in number. Their coverage has also risen. But inter-regional mobility takes a very long time to emerge. Even within a region, there are considerable obstacles towards mobility. In general, there has been a drift of employment seekers to the towns as reflected in slums in every city and town: mobility is greater among neighboring regions. Punjab has attracted labour from Uttar Pradesh and Rajisthan. Karnatka attracts labour from Kerala and Tamil Nadu. Metropolitan centres like Mumbai attracts talents from distant parts. In so far as the rural sector is concerned, the effect of a climate of mobility is yet to manifesto itself. In rural areas, particularly among self-employed families it is customary to maintain the unemployed as a part of households. Even the distinction between the employed and unemployed is blurred. This has actually enabled a larger number of relatives among cultivator families to be maintain within the household. It is an urban area where nuclear families are emerging particularly among the top income groups and in low income groups, sharing is common.

This is reflected in the very low room-pace among the middle and the low-income classes in the urban areas. It is fair to state that in the economy the unemployed are maintained by the employed households. It is in recent that some state Government have been small experimentations based on various launched schemes to contribute employment opportunity.

The problem of unemployment is truly gigantic: Since its true dimension does not get revealed, it is a sort of hidden time bomb. If we take into account the probable extent of disguised unemployment including the proportion of potential of labour force not revealing itself, as labour-force is unemployed and / or underemployed. The NSS 27th round had asked some probing questions as to how many of employed in certain classes would like to shift from their existing jobs and locations. The answers point to the proportion of such involuntarily disguised unemployment to the nearly 25 per cent of the labour-force. The estimate of the first Five Year Plan which estimated that about 30 per cent of the labour-force in India was unemployed may hold true even today. This accounts for the high measure of the merely 50 per cent of the population below the modest poverty line. The stability of the poverty-proportion through good and bad years is a pointer that the economic system so far has not made any sizeable dent upon the problem of unemployment and underemployment. In estimating yearly production of average of land and stock of other resources are found less than half per cent annum: the capital output ration is itself going up at a fast rate: and the rate of profit is showing a steeply falling tendency. What the relative share of wages at around 70 per cent of national income, if the capital-output ratio goes on moving up, the rate of profit is bound to go up and down. According to an econometric force cast, the Indian economy may reach a commodity-stationary state at around mid-90's if the present drift continues. That means that we have to make determined efforts to render the population since stationary before the actual commodity-stationary state sets in.

Whatever measures are necessary to reduce the proportion of unemployment that must be devised within the framework in the above perspective. Redistributional policies persee without severely restricting population growth would certainly be of no help under our present, circumstances. The scope for a framework of additional material incentives for different type of work, except at the level of ordinary labour, is also constrained. There is a room for considerable alterations in the pattern of investment with a greater emphasis for capacity to produce wage-goods. Improvident mechanization with no downward effect on the capital-output ratio is certainly not the best of the socially desired course. In view of the urgent need to bring down the capital-output ratio in every sphere of economic activity and to economize on the use of circulating capitals including raw materials, it is incumbent on the economy to adopt policies of greater labour mobility. This has its implications in the sphere of education and reservation of jobs. One thing is clear that under the Indian conditions, for a fairly long time to come, the components of economic policy will have to be radically different from those normally fashionable in the context of the unemployment problem in the Western countries. From the time of the industrial policy resolution of 1956 the government made extraordinary efforts in execution of climate and infrastructure introduced to a healthy growth of small-scale industrial sector. Technical assistance, financial arrangements, hire purchase schemes for machinery and materials, marketing assistance and even managerial- guidance have been provided as and when appropriate.

Licensing policy sought to promote to production of ancillaries in small and medium sized units by encouraging competent entrepreneurs. They have been encouraged to produce certain mass consumption goods as well.

As a consequence of these efforts the modern small units have become a distinctive feature of industrial development. A tangible result has been the substantial progress in the small scale sector with respect to output as well as employment generation.

However, it is felt in many quarters that the performance is not commensurate with expectations. One of the major indicators of the malady is the high input intensity despite the low capital intensity. In particular we note the following:

(a) The average cost of production in all units is Rs. 0.85 per rupee value of production in the case of large scale units.

(b) The working capital requirements are 43% of scales as against 27 per cent for large scale units,

(c) On the output front we observe that as against productivity per worker of the order of Rs. 5,991 in the large-scale sector we only have about Rs. 2,603 in the small scale units. Further, it has been observed that there is a negative correlation between capital intensity and productivity as reflected in the net value added per worker. Therefore, at least in some industries capital exists in a form not suited for efficient operation.

The SBI also found that in the case of some units the entrepreneur was in far to much hurry to build up fixed assets even at the expense of efficient current operations, this result in a failure to maintain the momentum. Thus, finding different references concerned with employment opportunity, Ahluwalia (1991) that consumer non-durable goods industries accounted for the bulk of the decline in employment in organised manufacturing in the first half of the 1980s. And that it is this group of industries, among various groups, which had the highest increased capital intensity as well as the maximum increase the real wage rate in the period.

Unorganised and Tiny Sector:

One of the peculiar paradoxes of the diversity in the manufacturing sector is the existence of a sizeable number of tiny and small units in the unorganised sector. There has been a large, though largely unsystematic, growth in these activities. Since they provide one of the major sources of employment we cannot ignore it altogether when we consider industrialization and employment.

There are various sources of such employment. One of the most important aspects is the non-agricultural sector within the traditional sector which includes mostly household enterprises in manufacturing trade and commerce, and services. Rural industrialization process created the other source —— popularly called the tiny sector with assets below Rs. 1 lakh. The rural industrial sector is very large in terms of employment.

Notwithstanding the importance of such activities in the economy, very little useful information exists which could be used to discard the trends in this sector.

Generally, one of the major complaints against the organised industrial sector has been the fact that the goods produced by it are largely confined to a predominantly urban elite while the majority of people do not have essential items of consumption. The production in the unorganised sector can be looked upon as a response to this trend. Secondly, the large number of artisans are widely dispersed geographically and their cultural diversity with the urban workers inhibits relocation and absorption into the urban sector. Even this phenomenon made it necessary that decentralized production occupy an important place.

Although special programmes were also initiated by the government with an emphasis on both production and employment generation, in practice. The main achievement has been the creation of employment opportunities without an adequate emphasis on the production aspect of employment generation or the productive function of the work programmes taken up. Perhaps the most important contribution has been that of an instrument of skill formation rather than immediate employment creation.

To be sure, this aspect of employment should not be underestimated. After all, as the new technology-even farm technology-makes the skills of the rural artisans obsolete, express attention is needed to train them in improved skills in a variety of interrelated trades so as to minimise the possible incidence of unemployment in the future.

There are, however, limits on the extent to which employment can be increased with additional capital formation in the traditional production lines. There is clearly a limit on the market demand for such goods. Hence, a diversification of products, appropriate choice of market makes, and even choice of technology is necessary to make further progress in the unorganised sector.

Papola (1978) observed that those activities of the informal sector which have shown good potential are significantly linked upto the markets of the organised sector. The growth of the organised sector may in the ultimate analysis set a limit on the growth prospects of the organised sector.

Linkages of Organised and Informal Sectors

We have so far been assuming that the organised private sector, the public sector, the organised small scale sector and the unorganised sectors are mostly insolated, self-sufficient and oriented to meeting specific types of final demand. Stated somewhat differently the assumption so far has been that very little of the output of any one of these sectors cross over to the other sectors.

However, the process of industrial development has been contributing to two kinds of changes. Firstly the production activities of the various sectors from a continuum with the boundaries between them blurred and overlapping. Secondly, they do tend to be mutually dependent. For example, there have been cross flows and use of inputs across the boundaries of two or more sectors. For example, the small scale sectors uses inputs from the large scale sectors. To converse is also true because the small-scale-sectors has been producing ancillaries to the large scale sector. These interrelationship and their effects on the patterns of employment are not systematically examined as yet.

In this regard, the following tables 2.4-2.7 provide evidences relating to, fixed assets employment and opportune capacity utilization in selected Small Scale Industries tiny and Small Units in the factory sectors, and information sector employment have been numerically studied in respective tables as shown below:

Table 2.4

Fixed Assets Employment and Output in small Sector by Broad Industry Groups

Industry	*Fixed assets Rs. Crores*	*Employment*	*Output Rs. Crores*
1. Food and beverages	61.43	1.37	159.69
2. Mosiery	36.11	0.75	155.43
3. Wood & paper products	129.43	1.84	2529.03
4. Leather & rubber products	91.87	1.14	239.73
5. Chemicals	100.92	1.59	346.65
6. Glass & Ceramics	62.87	2.02	125.52
7. Metal products	272.93	4.10	763.26
8. Machinery and parts	125.30	1.45	763.26
9. Electrical products	53.98	0.66	151.72
10.Others	119.87	1.63	220.75
Total	1054.71	16.55	2602.77

Source: Government of India, Report of the Study Team on Centre-State Relations, Administrative Reforms Commission, 1968, Vol. 1.

Table 2.5
Capacity Utilization In Selected Small Scale Industries

Industry	*Capacity Rs. Crores*	*Production Rs. Crores*	*Utilization Per cent*
1. Cotton knitwear	9.01	4.63	51
2. Saving of wood	7.30	3.03	41
3. Leather shoes	1.37	0.77	56
4. Paints & vernishes	5.71	2.76	48
5. Tiles	1.28	0.85	66
6. Steel casting & forgings	44.08	20.76	47
7. Fruits & bolts	4.25	1.93	45
8. Auto parts	11.72	6.21	53
9. Cycle parts	4.58	2.66	58
10. Tenning of leather	3.67	2.93	80

Source: *Ibid*. (Table 2.4).

Table 2.6
Tiny And Small Units In The Factory Sector

Description	*Capital Rs. Lakhs*	*Employment Lakhs*	*Output Rs. Lakhs*
1. Tiny	21.700	8.91	2,36,358
2. Small scale	91.640	20.37	6,82,293
3. Tiny/Small (x)	23.69	43.77	34.64
4. Tiny/Total factor Sector (percent)	1.55	13.97	7.91

Source: *Ibid* (Table2.4).

Table 2.7
Informal Sector Employment

Industry	Percent of informal Sector Employment	Percent of total Employment
1. Agriculture	6.75	4.00
2. Manufacturing	23.00	44.00
3. Construction	3.50	3.40

4. Trade and commerce	29.25	19.60
5. Transport & communications	12.25	7.40
6. Others services	25.25	21.60
Total	100.00	100.00

Source: Ibid (Table 2.4).

The most glaring interdependence has been the public sector and the organised private sector. And yet I know there is no study which deals with this aspect in detail. The link of the unorganised sector with the organised sector have generally remained weak. In certain cases, especially engineering goods, subcontracting from the organised sector appears to have been advantageous to the unorganised sector. But, by and large, the organised sector have only provided limited services to the unorganised sectors and that too at uneconomical rates.

Relationship Between Workforce and Industrial Society

For creating industrialized achievement in our society, the workforce to industrial employees is required of existence of the total knowledge, skills, creative abilities, talents and aptitudes among employed persons for obtaining maximum results from human resources. These developed and required components are not independently distributed because actions and reactions existing to workforces of employees are used for technological development. The development is meant in the exploitation of natural resources to the industrial society following considerable economics of the country.

In realization of human resources to fulfil the conditions of abilities of industrial employees, the planners and decisions makers have stressed on utilization of human resources following exploitation of natural resources. These policies have been exhaustively studied by them since independence of the country. Believing such examploy situations, many institutions have been set up since then for the training and development of human resources such as; All India council of Technical Education in 1949, National Council for Educational Research and Training in 1956, National Productivity Council in 1958, Small Industries Extension Training Institute in 1962 and also other institution like Indian council of Agricultural Research, Indian Institute of Technology, Indian Institute of Mines, Institute of Mines, Institute of Economic

Growth, and Institutes of Management, etc. The perspective features of these institution emphasise on education, training and research and also health and nutrition to create balanced growth among employees of both limited and leading industries.

The three mentioned factors have been considerable in the constitution of India, when Independence of the country has come into force as a federal state. However, it seems that the constitution has given powers to the center for providing balanced economy in creation of secular democratic norms as well as development process in elimination of linguistic, communal and religions factors. Because these components associated to the traditional societies of our country did make any initiation in strengthening capabilities of employees of industrial society.

Further, referring to different Indian plans, the following operational goals have been considered for mixed economy of the country:

(i) to achieve an increase in the national income;

(ii) to achieve desired levels of investment/income ratio;

(iii) to reduce inequalities of income and concentration of economic power;

(iv) to generate additional employment opportunities.

The worth of stated ingredients could be included in the technique in the techniques planning in case of industry-agriculture linkages. Therefore, the planner were not able to provide considerable targets for the private sectors in terms of investment outlays. Also, there has also not been possible for them to provide plan targets in spatial terms.

The plan accepted that development of regions and national economy as a whole have to be viewed as a part of a single process" and that the ultimate objective" must be that over a reasonable period all regions in the country should realize their potential for economic development and should attain level of living not far removed from to those of the nation as a whole (Planning Commissio, 1961, *op. cit.* p. 153).

The Planning Commission (1961) realized the claims of under developed regions for extending better employment opportunity to persons of under developed areas within short span of time by creating infrastructural facilities during the plan periods. Though the First and Second Five Year Plans did not have any explicit policy relating to balanced regional development in respect of employment growth to the industrial spheres.

However, the fifth five year plan (1974-79), for the first time planner accepted that there need not to be a trade-off between national growth and reduction of regional inequalities. Stressing on development of backward regions, there was made a great realization of impotance of growth employment in industries. In this regard the view was taken to increase the level of living of the lowest 30 percent of the population of the backward regions (Planning commission Draft Outline – Fifth Five Year Plan, Government of India, New Delhi, 1973, pp. 31-33).

Based on Draft outline, the National Committee on the Development of Backward Areas, there have been proposed the following incentives:

(a) capital subsidy (during construction stage of the project;

(b) interest subsidy during intitial stages of the production; and

(c) tax subsidy after the successful operation of the project.

The mentioned conditions were considered by the National Committee for the reasons of drought prove areas, desert areas, hill areas, tribal areas, chronically flood affected areas and costal areas affected by salinity as referred by the committee (1980, 13).

Further, for growth of employment to persons, belonging to backward regions showed the following conditions of the population for recognizing the regions: (a) they should have population of 50,000 or more, (b) they should have less than 10,000 workers in non-household manufacturing, and (c) they should not be near the existing industrial centers.

In contest of regional imbalance existing in the country, there did not appear proportionate employment apportunities to us in industrial sectors that caused unadapted growth of employment to persons of the country in industrial sectors. Therefore in our country, it would seem that the characteristics of asymmetry would be prevalent, due to existence of regional diversities in terms of culture, history, language and levels of development. These characteristics of asymmetry must have gained strength with the linguistic recognisation of the states.

Because, at the time of Independence of the country, the cultural diversities and related geographical factors made federalism inevitable. There emerged a federation "in which the paramountary British Government had over Indian princely states (taken over the Union Government and applied to all units), mentioned, Dikshit, 1971. Spatial disparities reduced by implementation of licences to industrial units.

In relation to industrial licences, there existed center-state Relations endorsed by the National Committee. This committee showed that it was much easier to settle issues between center and states, when the congress partly was ruling simultaneously at the center and states levels. But the emergence of non-congress state assemblies increased the tensions. The committee cited the examples of Kerala, Tamil Nadu and west Bengal (referred in Study Team on Centre-State Relations, Administrative Reforms Commission, 1968, Vol. 1).

In consideration of administrative set up for the central government could influence the spread of industrial sectors in three following different ways:

(a) some changes in the location could be achieved through government regulations, incentives and policies (industrial policy fiscal policy and price controls;

(b) changes in the spatial pattern which might result from the state ownership and controls of industries (public sectors); and

(c) there could belocational changes which occurred as a by-product of government policies not directly intended to change industrial location.

Thus, these inducement of various forms of incentives provided extended control over diversities for locational devision (Harcourt, 1968, pp. 77-95).

Further, the stated incentives concerning linked prosperity between agriculture-industry provided several kinds of impact on the industrial sectors such as, (i) in the form of supply of wage goods, (ii) in the form of increased supply of raw-materials, and (iii) as a potential market for industrial products. These components could provide a great deal of employment in the industrial sectors corresponded to initiated avenues to industrial workforces but followed by the industrial licensing policy between center and states. This policy could achieve balanced economic development of different regions and the contry and played significant role in the country and played significant role in altering the spatial pattern of industrialization that gave greater opportunity to the industrial workers in respect of employment.

For example of Bhilai located in Madhya Pradesh and selected by Russian technicians that could fulfill the government's edeological and political objectives in 1954 as mentioned by Johnson (1966). Such industrial location for stated enterprise contributed greater approach to the growth of employment in the industrial sector.

Similarly, Johnson (1966) remarked that the British Mission that visited India in 1955, was shown location in only two states west Bengal and Bihar. He indicated that when Durgapur in West Bengal was selected for British mill it was announced that the next public sector plant would be situated in Bihar at Bokaro.

Also, in concentration of growth of employment to persons of West Bengal, this state itself created extra pressure on the central government of locating the steel mill in its region. The proclaimed plan of the state Government built a mill and then a coke even battery at Durgapur. Around the time the center finalized the location of British Mill at Durgapur, sufficient popular support had been created in West Bengal for location at Duragpur. These forces might have played an important role in the location of other public sector plants also such role contributed greater approach toward growth of employment and treated as extended workforce in industrial sector of the state.

Obviously, planning commission was not found in inclination of providing spatial distribution of industrial targets. The process of licensing was completely left to devide the spatial distribution of industrial licences to potential states of the country as industrial licensing policy had on objective to achieve "balance economic development" indicated by Hazari in year 1967. It was supposed to influence the optimum size of project, time phasing and location of the project with the assistance of Directorate General for Trechnical Development (D.G.T.D.). But due to the absence of any criteria for giving weight to alternative objectives of the policy, in the grant and rejection of industrial licences, accompanied by poor quality of techno. Economic studies of the proposed investment, conducted by D.G.T.D.

Thus it was licencing policy that made initiation of influencing of the industrial project to the industrial sectors (public sectors) but not to the private sectors. Such initiation of establishing projects in different states of the country provided increased trend of employment growth.

Having observed, Dutt Committee admitted that the licencing system could not much assist the industrially backward regions, because the number of proposals. For locating industrial units in the states there was much smaller proportion of licenses to set up industrial units as pointed by Dutt. Such comment given by Dutt, there did not make any influence in closing spatial location for establishing projects. However, persuasion of great demand of the people of different states of the country, there could be recognized more for establishing project to utilize manpowers, in manufacturing industrial products. This establishment followed increased trend of employment apportunity to persons belonging to respective states.

Table 2.9

Ranking of State in Terms of Net State Domestic Product (NSDP) (RY) 1951-1981

Sl.No.	State	1971	1981	1991	2001 Projected
1.	Andhra Pradesh	9	6	7	9
2.	Assam	10	10	14	10
3.	Bihar	14	14	14	14
4.	Gujarat	2	3	5	5
5.	Karanataka	5	5	6	6
6.	Kerala	6	8	8	9
7.	Madhya Pradesh	13	12	12	13
8.	Maharashtra	3	2	1	2
9.	Orissa	11	13	14	15
10.	Punjab	1	1	1	2
11.	Rajasthan	7	9	10	12
12.	Tamil Nadu	8	8	7	9
13.	Uttar Pradesh	12	11	11	12
14.	West Bengal	4	4	3	4

Source: Central Statistical Organization, National Account Statistics, Government of India (various years).

The states Assam, Madhya Pradesh, Orissa and U.P. followed highest rank among other ten remaining states of the country in respect of net domestic product.

Sum up

All said and done we cannot escape the conclusion that the growth in the volume of investment is still the most important single determinant of employment in all forms of organisation. Choice of techniques themselves would have a very limited role to play. In almost al the sectors and for almost all products we have been witnessing the coexistence of many techniques. This pattern will continue to persist even in the future and trying to pin down any one technique as optimal would be totally out of place. It is much more important to realize that the structural features of labour-force, and not necessarily economic criteria such as surplus generated etc., are the primary determinants of choice of techniques. It may also be noted that the strikingly different patterns of skill will not change from a long time to come. Employment practices in the past adjusted to these and will have to continue doing so. The added problem is the obsolescence of traditional skills and there is a need to up-date, if industry does not want to suffer from the lack of skilled man power in their quest for further expansion.

The diversities in the organizational forms, such as privates sectors, public sector came about for specific economic reasons and they have complementary roles to play. It is important that they function as such instead of considering each other as interrelationship between the various sectors. No usable information is available at this stage. Purely in terms of employment generation, emphasis on output maximization either through better capacity utilization or otherwise is misplaced.

Even when there is an increase in output it is important to realise that the saving and investment potential must be harnessed and re-channeled into appropriate investments. It will be rather difficult to define the appropriate mix of products in the abstract. They must be looked upon as an evolutionary process. It is necessary to study the impact of various fiscal policies on employment generation. However, it should be clearly recognized that no. simple form of market intervention and price mechanism will channel investments in the desired direction. Industrial licensing and allotting priorities for production in different sectors is a necessary evil.

The most important aspect that we noticed is that production of universal intermediates-particularly electricity generation and generating new employment. This should be looked at not from the view point of direct employment but the menacing impact on indirect employment. For some reason the government policy lost sight of this after having considered the universal intermediates as a prime over earlier.

Exports, both traditional and modern, have shown significant employment possibilities for even the lower level of skills. Maintaining this in the face of international competition may be one of the foremost prerequisites. One last point of paramount importance remains to be sated. A great deal of justifiable investment is going on in the small-scale sector but generally the managerial processes are so inefficient that the sector as a whole is far from regenerative. The sooner we pay attention to this sector, in terms of sustaining and improving the employment potential of this sector, the more we stand to gain.

Analysis of the nature of the mixed economy and the strategy of regional planning clearly establishes that the core of the planning process in India has continue' to be intersectoral in character. To achieve regional equity, government relied on ad hoc committees and working grups. These ad hoc bodies evolved criteria for the identification of backward regions and also suggested suitable strategies for developing these regions.

Throughout the planning period the government policies were based on the assumptions; (a) that the development of infrastructural facilities in different regions will pari pasu lead to spatial spread of industrialization: and (b) the development policies of small-scale industries will correct the regional imbalances created by the spatial concentration of large-scale plants.

The anatomy of the changing nature of federalism suggests that the lingusistic recognization of state boundaries resulted in increasing regional pulls and pressures. However, until 1967, due to the continuous hegemony of the Congress Party at the center and in the states, policy reflected the characteristics of a unitary state. After 1967, regional pressures were quite significant and resulted in the supremacy of the National Development Council over the Planning Commission.

The empirical results regarding the spatial distribution of public-sector investment suggest that, until 1970, public sector investment favoured materials-rich industrially backward states. This bias in public-sector investment can be explained partly with the help of the development strategy of materials-oriented industry during this period, and partly by the state's deliberate attempt to achieve regional dispersal. However, after 1970, due to changes in the composition of investment in favour of market-oriented industries and the increasing role of regional pressures, public-sector investment assumed a wider spatial spread but this development was relatively more favourable to already industrialized states.

The licensing policy, which was expected to play a significant role in the spatial spread of industries, could not achieve its objective of regional dispersal. The empirical results clearly show that the spatial distribution of licenses followed the same pattern as was observed in the case of the spatial pattern of industrialization.

References

1. National Committee (1980), *op. cit.*, p. 13.
2. R.D. Dikshit, "Iafluence of Government System on Location of Economic Activity" in G.J.R. Linge and P.J. Rimmer (eds.), Government Influence of Location of Economic Activity, Australian National University, 1971, pp. 163-133).
3. Government of India, Report of the Study Team on Centre-State Relations, Administrative Reforms Commission, 1968, Vol.1
4. G.C. Harcourt, Investment Decision Criteria Investment Incentives and Choice of Technique, Economic Journal, Vol. 78, (1968), pp.77-95.
5. William A. Johnson, Steel Industry of India, Harward University Press, U.S.A., 1966, p.188.
6. R.K. Hazari, Industrial Planning and Licensing Policy, Planning Commission, Government of India, 1967, p. I, see also, Ninth Report of the Extimates Committee, IV Lok Sabha, Lok Sabha Secretariat, 1967.
7. Dutt Committee (1969), *op.cit.*, 114.

3

Evolution of Extended Industrial Process In The Country

For examining the trend of employment the light is given to the industrial development of the country following different five years plans. The approach of India's Five Year Plans towards the problems of unemployment appears to be hit out over a sufficient period when intensive development of the economy had been undertaken such as, ((i) capital formation at a rapid rate, (ii) provision of 'employment, (iii) consistent goals between industrial output and employment opportunity emphasizing adaptations and shifts during the production process for admitting certain special situations.

In order to have an approach of the study of different Five Year Plans, the First Five Year did not show evidence for problems of unemployment considerations. It dress attention to the distinction between advanced countries, where full employment was not possible on account of lack of adequate supplies of cooperating factors such as land and equipment. Though this plan could stress on approach of economic and industrial priorities for which the total out lay was Rs.180 crores in 1953. Though the out lay specified" for financing new schemes "that would simultaneously expand employment potential. The potentiality of employment might be grown by consideration of labour intensive projects like small industries, road transport, etc: These programmes were included in mentioned Plan to make maximum use of idle labour, and (b) for increasing employment at rising levels of real income under certain limitations. Therefore this plan has been recommended as steady plan in throwing light for elimination of existing unemployment situation prevailing in the country.

Thus, the First Plan Period showed an open of some fresh awareness of employment but on the whole it did not amount to much since the very approach of the Plan was modest and theoretically not employment oriented.

But the second Plan therefore, laid greater stress on the problem of unemployment and underemployment by means of enunciation of rapid industrialization. Though in this plan period, a separate entity of unemployment situation in the country was not given. In this plan period, "employment" has been considered in determination of pattern of investment by making understand of optimum scale of investment emphasisng to the development of large scale joint stock industrial enterprises on the one hand and village and small industries on the other. From such investment, there aroused employment content in an indication of full employment, labour-intensive technique surplus generated per person in a labour intensive technique.

Thus, the Second Five Year Plan could also recognize the expanded employment as an integral part of the Plan throwing the light on professed standpoint of employment opportunities in various heavy industries of the country.

The Third Plan emphasized the increasing utilization of labour in construction projects, imparting of suitable skills, fuller utilization of small industries and programmes of rural industrialization, rural electrification, etc that resulted significant results of employment opportunities based on following factors:

(a) shift in the occupational distribution;

(b) Larger employment programmes under taken into development programmes;

(c) Effective utilization of rural manpower, and

(d) Determining continued process of trend for larger proportion of the employment opportunities, depending on both agriculture and industry.

The Fourth Plan showed an attribute of repeated process for those objectives existing in the Third Plan concerning employment opportunities under the following conditions:

(i) balanced aptitude between development and employment considerations in consequence of shaped planning;

(ii) larger gains of employment from perspective development programmes undertaken by determination of corrected attention and the use of local resources in implementation of small scale industries in villages; and

(iii) adaption of development policies and priorities emerging in certain categorised forms of workers engaged in industries for over a long period.

Thus the Fourth Five Year Plan emphasised in indicating extended form of employment opportunities by means of effective utilisation of existing productive capacities highest level of feasibility, substantial growth in economy and fighting against scourage of unemployment and underemployment criteria in both rural and urban sectors of the country.

The Fifth Plan provided great emphasis to the assistance of employment opportunities in finding achievement and objective of the employment opportunities subject to the condition of existing intensity, efforts and potentiality and capability work with the context of environmental understandings of fiscal measures in relation to larger scale of unemployment and underemployment.

In the Fifth Plan period, there has been pointed out that it is not necessary that large scale industries would solve all required problems concerning employment opportunities, rather employment might be undertaken in view of consideration of development of agriculture and industrial investments – as most effective, measures in reducing unemployment consideration both rural and urban sectors, in particular to rural sectors. But this possible only when large scale industries are being built up to absorb more effective employment.

Reviewing al the five successive plan in our country, there is found greater relationship between employment and growth of outputs. These outputs provided raised trends of absorbed employment opportunities in the volume of employment.

Labour force in an indication of age structure

The growth rate of employment opportunity can be determined partly by the age structure of the population of the country following age structure, which is presented in the table 3.1 for specific periods 1997-2002.

Table 3.1

Distribution of Age Structure of Population : 1997-2002

Percent

Age group	1997	2002
0-14	37.23	59.41
15-59	56.07	59.41
60+	6.70	7.00

Source: The Indian Journal of Labour Economics Employment Perspective, Vol.42, No.1 1999, p.115.

The figures, shown in the table 3.1, have provided the age profile of the Ninth Plan period which is likely to witness a sharp decline in the share of the population in the age group of 0 to 14 years, and a corresponding increase in the age group of 15 to 56 years, with the 60+ age group more or less retaining its share.

In connection with age structure, the further investigation for six composition (male and female) who have participated in their respective works to both rural and urban sectors to the period 1977-94. This study would reveal constituent share in labour force participated by both sexes as given in the following table 3.2 pated by both sexes as given in the following table 3.2 foo obtaining trend values in labour force participation rates.

Table 3.2

Trends in Labour Force Participation Rates

Per thousand of population.

Age Group	*Period*	*Male*		*Female*	
		Rural	*Urban*	*Rural*	*Urban*
15-29	1977-78	879	746	515	257
	1987-88	824	710	478	211
	1993-94	804	684	455	204
30-44	1977-78	990	990	619	324
	1987-88	988	987	603	301

(Contd...)

(Contd...)

	1993-94	990	986	600	300
45-59	1977-78	963	940	538	291
	1987-88	964	933	538	275
	1993-94	968	937	543	283
60+	1977-78	667	517	221	130
	1987-88	670	482	220	123
	1993-94	699	443	241	114
All (15+)	1977-78	904	831	517	269
	1987-88	879	810	496	239
	1993-94	877	811	491	238

Note : Copnstituent shares in labour force in 1993-94 are Rural Male : 0. 499, Rural Female : 0.270, Urban Male. 1.182 and urban Female : 0.049

Source : Same as Table 3.1.

The emperical study in table 3.2 provides variaties in labour force participation rates (LFPR) during the past 16 year – period are not uniform across age groups: there is a substantial decline in LFPR in the age group 15-29; practically no change in 30-44 years, and a slight increase in the higher age groups.

In consideration of the same structure, participation age structure, participation in labour fore in differentiation of six for the period 1997-2012 has been made for knowing trend values in it for inferring the value in practical age group me 40-44 in the following table 3.3: participation in labour force by Age Group and by Sex : 1977-2012.

Table 3.3

(per thousand of Population)

Age	*Males*				*Females*			
	1977	*2002*	*2007*	*2012*	*1997*	*2002*	*2007*	*2012*
15-19	517	482	447	412	302	282	261	241
20-24	871				408			
25-29	975				454			

(Contd...)

(Contd...)

30-34	988		505	
35-39	990		526	
40-44	986	(a)	538	(b)
45-49	981		524	
50-54	961		476	
55-59	914		411	
60+	637			

Note: (a) No change in labour force participation in age groups above 20 years.

To have the concept of trend value in labour force participation to specific period of age 30-34 during the Ninth Plan, the following study eveals projected value for 2002 to follow percentage of growth of labour force when age group of the population of the country is considered there. This study has comprised in the following table 3.4.

Table 3.4
Labour Force Projections By Age Groups

(Million)

Age group	*Million*		*Growth (% p.a)*
	1997	2002	
15-19	40.31	45.03	2.24
20-24	55.45	62.91	2.51
25-29	56.89	61.47	1.56
30-34	52.64	58.88	2.26
35-39	46.60	52.80	2.53
40-44	39.56	46.04	3.08
45-49	82.90	8.13	2.99
50-54	25.86	30.27	3.20
55-59	18.86	2.45	3.55
60+	28.15	31.64	2.37
15+	397.22	449.62	2.51

Source : The Indian Journal Labour Economics, Vol. 42.

On the basis of the age and sex structure of the population based on the information pertaining to 1987-88 and 1993-94 NSS and the 1991 census, the labourforce is projected to increase by 52.4 million during the ninth Plan period an usual status. Concept, as provided in the above table 3.4. As may be seen, the absolute number of persons in the age group 35-60 age group of labour force increases sharply during the Ninth Plan because of the change in the age picture, which leads to a percent or higher growth rate in the labour force comprising persons in the age group, 40, 55 despite an expected reduction in the LFPR of this age group.

Estimates of Elasticity of Employment.

This study is based on relationship between employment and output: (i) estimates of employment and unemployment prepared in the basis of allocation of times by an individual in differentiated activities for different sectors; and (ii) estimates of output made using national income concepts. For such estimate, data for the former is collected through quinquennial National Sample Suneys and for the latter through the system of National Accounts. Although there are some conceptual differences between the two sources of data, they can be used so long as the differences remain consistent overtime. The relationship between the two variables, i.e. output and employment, at the sectoral level has varied overtime, but has been observed to have remained within a reasonable range if the effects of economic shocks, such as droughts, are accounted for.

However, with an econometric approach, the elasticity ot employment can be estimated by considering some margin of error at different sect oral tends as provided in the following table 3.5 for actual periods 1972-94 and projected period 1997 2002.

Table 3.5

Elasticity of Employment of GDP

Sector	Employment Elasticity					
	1972-73 to 1977-78	1977-78 to 1983	1983 to 1987-88	1987-88 to 1993-94	1983 to 1993-94	1997 to 2002
		Actual			Projected	
1. Agriculture	0.75	0.45	0.45	0.53	0.50	0.50
2. Mining and quarrying	0.94	0.80	1.00	0.39	0.67	0.60

3. Manufacturing	1.00	0.67	0.29	0.42	0.33	0.25
4. Electricity	1.00	0.73	0.73	0.33	0.50	0.50
5. Construction	0.33	1.00	1.00	0.00	1.00	0.60
6. Wholesale & retail trade	1.00	0.78	0.63	0.59	0.60	0.555
7. Tpt. Storage & Communication	0.74	1.00	0.25	0.68	0.47	0.55
8. Financing, real estate, insurance & business services	0.00	1.00	0.11	1.00	0.90	0.53
9. Community, Social and personal services	0.73	0.83	0.27	0.92	0.59	0.50
All Sectors	0.59	0.53	0.38	0.43	0.40	0.38

The figures following in the above table 3.5 have provided the elasticity of employment on a sector basis which can then be utilized for projecting employment both at the sectoral and at the aggregate level for the Ninth Plan. But these elasticity estimated as obtained in the table which need to be recognized that these estimates can change depending upon the economic structure and competition of growth at the sub-sectoral level.

In light of sectoral level, projections of work opportunities for specific periods may be undertaken into consideration as;

Table 3.6

Projections of Work Opportunities 1997-2002

Sector	*GDP Growth (% p.a) 2002 (million 1997)s*	*work opportunities 1997*	*2002*
1. Agriculture	3.9	238.32	262.48
2. Mining & quarrying	7.2	2.87	3.54
3. Manufacturing	8.2	43.56	48.22
4. Electricity	9.3	1.54	1.93
5. Construction	4.9	14.74	17.03
6. Whole sale & retail trade	6.7	34.78	41.67
7. Transport, storage and communication	7.3	11.96	14.57

8. Financing, real estate, insurance and Business services	8.5	4.55	5.68
9. Community, social and Personal Services	7.1	38.98	46.41
All Sector	6.5	391.30	441.52

The figures presented in the above table 3.6 showed 6.5 per cent annum on an average for existing showed growth target for Ninth Plan. The sectoral structure of growth corresponding to 6.5 per cent growth in GDP along with the estimated sectoral elasticities, yield an increase in work opportunities during the mentioned plan period.

In consideration of labour force and employment during the two plan periods Eighth (1992-97) and Ninth (1997-2002) plans, the following table 3.7 provides rate percent of rated (million) for three ingredients indicating the projection of labour forceand work opportunities created during the Ninth Plan leading a reduction in the average rate of unemployment during the Ninth Plan period compared to the Plan.

Table 3.7

Distribution of Labour Force and Employment in Eigth and Ninth Plan Periods

(Million)

Classified work to the population	Eigth Plan (1992-97)	Ninth Plan (1997-2002)
Labour force	374.2	423.4
Employment	367.2	416.4
Unemployment	7.0	7.0
(rate) (Percent)	(1.87)	(1.66)

Note: Estimates have been made based on mentioned tables 3.1-3.6.

Source: The Indian Journal of Labour Economics: Documentation Vol. 42, No. 1.

January-March, 1999, p. 120.

For creating full employment in the post-plan period, the labour force growth is expected to be at its peak in the Ninth Plan period.

But attainment of near full employment by the year 2007 may not be unreasonable target provided that the conditionsare created for further acceleration in the growth rate and the intensity of labour absorption is not substantially reduced both sectorally and in terms of the sectoral structure of growth.

In this context, the following table 3.8 gives an idea of unemployment rate (per cent) till the 10th Plan period (2002-07) – a projected value for labour force, employment and unemployment ingredients stating as annual averages during the plan period.

Table 3.8

Population, Labour Force and Employment

(Million)

Classified with to the population	*1978 (a)*	*1983 (b)*	*1994 (a)*	*8th Plan (1992-97) (f)*	*9th Plan (1997-02) (f)*	*Total Plan (2002-07) (f) projected*
Population ©	637.6	718.2 (2.19)	895.0 (2.12)	9951.2 (1.89)	1028.9 (1.58)	1112.9 (1.58)
Labour force	2558	286.6 (2.09)	368.5 (2.42)	374.2	423.4	478.8
Employment	249.1	281.2	361.5	367.2	416.4	74.7 (d)
Unemployment	6.7	5.4	7:0	7.0	7.0	4.1 (e)
Unemployment rate (%)	2.63	1.89	1.89	1.87	1.66	0.86 (e)

Note: 1. Estimates of labour force and employment are an annual status concept and pertain to 15 years and above.

2. Figures in brackets are compound growth the rates in the preceeding period.

(a) As on 1st January.

(b) As on 1st July.

(c) Population at the terminal year of the plan.

(d) Required to attain near full employment.

(e) Unemployment reduces to negligible level by the year 2007.

(f) Labour force, employment and unemployment are started as annual averages during the plan period.

Source: The Indian Journal of Labour Economics, Documentations, Vol. 42, No.1.

January-March, 1999, p. 121.

The mentioned above table 3.8 percents gives unemployment rate 1.66 and 0.86, during the 9th Plan (1997-02) and 10th Plan respectively as projected there.

Attainment of employment and labour force during Ninth Plan (1997-2002) and Tenth Plan (2002-2007) in different major states of the country.

It is obvious that the balance between labour force and employment oportunities in the country will vary across the regions. Over the perspective period, 1997-2012, labour force will be rising at an increasing or at a decreasing pace depending upon two factors, viz. (a) the time at which changes in fertility have occurred in the respective states, and (b) the need and willingness of people to participate in or withdraw from the labour force. It is therefore possible to estimate the regional dispersion in the growth of the labour force on the basis of the available demographic data and State-specific LFPR. This problem is seemed as difficult due to reason of work opportunities. While a regional employment growth profile consistent with the targeted aggregate and sectoral GDP growth in the Ninth Plan cannot be projected using the available data or the plan model, it is possible to have some indication of trends in regional employment situation under specific assumptions. If the disparties in aggregate economic growth rates of each state relative to the growth rate of GDP is assumed to be the same as experienced during the period 1983-1994, and further if quality of employment in terms of labour productivity continues to be the same, yielding stable relationships between the growth in state domestic products and creation of work opportunities, on a state-wise basis for the Ninth Plan period. Under these assumptions, the growth rates of the labour force and of work opportunities on a state-wise basis have esp estimated and presented in the following table 3.9 in an indication of employment growth (under assumption) and labour force growth for both 9th and 10th Plans to different major states of the country.

Table 3.9

Distributions of Employment Growth (1997-02) Under Assumption of Unchanged Trend in Inter-state Disparities in Economic Growth and Growth in Labour Force (1997-02 and 2002-07) – Major States

State	Employment growth under stated assumptions	Labour Force Growth	
	1997-2002	1997-2002 (Percent per annum)	2002-2007 projected
All India	2.44	2.51	2.47
Andhra Pradesh	3.11	2.39	2.34
Assam	3.73	2.73	2.79
Bihar	1.29	2.58	2.85
Gujaart	2.53	2.37	2.18
Haryana	3.49	2.99	2.84
Karnataka	2.81	2.47	2.26
Kerala	1.26	2.30	1.90
Madhya Pradesh	2.61	2.39	2.48
Maharashtra	2.54	2.26	2.20
Orissa	2.35	2.10	2.13
Punjab	0.73	2.27	2.08
Rajasthan	2.71	2.84	2.91
Tamil Nadu	2.00	1.98	1.70
Uttar Pradesh	2.07	2.57	2.68
West Bengal	2.75	2.52	2.45

Source: The Indian Journal of Labour Economics: Documentation, Vol.42, No.1, January-March 1999, p.131.

By means of projection for two mentioned plan periods 9th and 10th Plans, there may be stated that of the 15 major states, 9 states are likely to experience a reduction in unemployment while 6 states may witness an increase. In the event that some of the states which record a decline in unemployment may have an existing unemployment base of less than the decrease indicated, it would indicate that an excess demand for workers may exists, which could be met either by the migration process from one state to another. It is unlikely, however that the patern of migration would be such as to entirely fill the supply shortages since migrations depends not only upon the level of information available to the unemployed regarding employment opportunities, but also on the skill profile required by the receiving states.

Further, an interpretation may be made that of the 6 states where unemployment is likely to increase Punjab, Kerala and Tamil Nadu are special in the sense that the minimum wage in these states is much higher than most of other states. The workers in those states expect better earning levels. A large proportion of the unemployed here can find better employment in other states gives better skills and training. Better information availability may facilitate their movement. In other three states; Bihar, Rajasthan and Uttar Pradesh; however, there conditions are unlikely to be fulfilled, and without active government intervention it is not possible to attain full creation of employment to provide workers concerned with job creation, initiation of labour force and common labour mobility.

In order to consider decent work as a development objective let us first briefly review the historical content Development objectives that reflect political, cultural, social and economic perception and these change over time. In 1950s and 1960s, the dominant goals of development were expressed in terms of industrialisation and modernisation. In dualistic economies, the growth of the modern industrial sector would provide the motor for development absorbing labour supply from traditional and rural sectors.

By the 1970s, the attention had turned to employment and inequality. It was perceived that economic growth and track down alone would not suffice to overcome problems of poverty and unemployment. Employment was seen in a mainly instrumental sense to that is to say, although work was also an objective in its own sight its main purpose was to generate both production and income, as a means of distributing the benefits of development more widely this led to the ILO's basic needs strategy, which was an attempt to reorient development towards satisfying the basic needs of the population as a whole through policies on both supply and demand sides. Basic needs went beyond income and employment public goods and participations.

In the 1980s, faced with persistent economic crisis and structural problems in low growth in the world economy, development goals were made subordinate to structural adjustment. A return to growth, it was argued, depended on fiscal orthodoxy, market reforms and investment in human capital. By the 1990s, the

World Bank's Development Report made the case in combined form that attempted to rout out poverty alleviation.

But by the early 1990, there is widespread concern about the slow pace of overall economic and social progress. Though the United Nations global conferences took the debates–Environment in Rio in 1992, Human Rights in Vienna in 1993 and Population and development in Cairo in 1994. These conferences threw light on massive mobilisation of the global community based on rights and justice, participation and equity, healthy environment, social integration and also employment.

During the period, Amartya Sen's book *'Development as Freedo'* (1999) has provided conception of development essentially meant for the expended freedoms that embrace political, social and economic goals. These freedoms in Sen's vision have a threefold relationship with development. Firstly, as goals in their own right (constitutive); secondly, because they contribute to the achievement of other valued goals such as security or social integration; and thirdly in the definition and building consensus around social needs, values and priorities (Constructive).

This interaction between freedoms and development is an important aspect of the rational for decent work as a development goal. Decent work brings together with different types of freedoms using Sen's terminology workers rights, income security, employment opportunities. These are goals in their own rights but taken together they are more than the sum of the parts whereby both social and economic factors are involved. And the decent work approach attempts to bring them together and to set them within a coherent framework.

Perspectives of Decent Work

The nation of decent work as a perspective aims to capture the aspects of work which are important for people. There are four main dimensions (i) Work and employment itself; (ii) Rights at work; (iii) Security; and (iv) Representation and dialogue.

The first dimension concerns work itself. Almost everyone works in one way or the other although much of this work may not be adequately recognised or rewarded. There are questions of both quantity and quality. People need to have enough work notably as a source of income. There are 160 million people in the world today who are unemployed (ILO estimates). But it is not enough to have work; we also have to take into account the content of this work and the conditions under which it is performed. This may radically affect its contribution to the personal goals of the workers concerned. The employment goal is best expressed as adequate opportunities for productive and meaningful work in decent conditions that means we have to take into account working time and work intensity the need for a living income, the possibilities for personal development and the opportunities to use one's capabilities. It includes formal and informal work, in the home, in the factory, or in the street. It includes women and men—much work by women, especially in the home, is undervalued or invisible. Women are better educated and hold more jobs world-wide than ever before. But they are heavily over–represented in precarious jobs, and they rarely break through the so-called glass ceiling separating them from top-level management and professional positions (ILO, 1997). Decent work may also mean not working too much or the possibility of retirement. Within the concept of decent work there is a broader notion of the place of work in life—so freedom from excessive work is an objective as well.

Employment and Unemployment Generation to Major Economic Activities of India

For employment generation, we study annual average rate of growth of real GDP in India for determination of highest and lowest level of increase / decrease in employment considerations adapting the following.

(a) Annual Average Rate of Growth (AARG).

This study has been made for different 6 sectors (Table 3.10) to different periods since 1981-82.

The study reveals AARG that the entire economy during the 1990s was higher, but only marginally so, in comparison with the corresponding rate during the 1980s. This some what higher rate of economic growth rate during in the 1990s also did make any dent in the mass. Unemployment figures. In fact, it was accompanied by the historically lowest rate of increase in employment during the 1990s. It should also be noted that the AARG in different sectors has been uneven. It has been lower in the 1990s as compared to the 1980s in potentially employment–intensive active such as agriculture, forestry, logging, mining and manufacturing. Consequently, as the Approach Paper to the Tenth Five Y ear Plan confesses, "Growth in the 1990s has generated less employment than was expected" (Planning Commission, 2001, p. 1).

Table 3.10
Annual Average Rate of Growth of Real GDP at Factor Cost by Sector of Origin (1993-94) (Percentages)

Sector	*1981-82 to 1985-86*	*1986-87 to 1990-91*	*1991-92 to 1995-96*	*1996-97 to 1999-00*
1. Entire Economy	4.94	6.00	5.36	6.50
2. Agriculture, forestry, logging fishing, mining and quarrying	3.46	4.22	2.64	3.67
3. Manufacturing, construction, electricity, gas and water supply	5.98	7.98	6.3	5.5
4. Transport, communication and trade	5.74	5.88	7.78	7.65
5. Banking, insurance, real estate, etc.	9.56	10.28	8.96	9.27
6. Public administration, defence, etc.	5.6	6.6	4.36	9.9

Source: Ministry of Finance, Government of India (GOI), Economic Survey, 2000-01, p. S-4, and S. 10.

Two things are worth remembering in this context. The economic growth has the "Spread effect" as well as the "backwash effect" on employment, and determining which of these effects is stronger would depend on the choice of technology. Similarly a significantly higher rate of economic growth such as 10 to 12 per cent per annum howsoever desired by everyone, would most likely remain an unachieved target in the near future.

Further, to concentrate on notable changes, the following Tables 3.11 and 3.12 have been asserted for sectoral and aggregate employment elasticity employees activities in the public and private sectors. The change has been made in manufacturing community social and personal services transport and communication and plantation and forestry emerging greater employment generation.

Table 3.11
Sectoral and Total Employment Elasticity of Growth in India, 1977-78 to 2002

Sector	1970-78 to 1983	1983 to 1987-88	1987-88 to 1993-94	1997 to 2002 (Project)
1. Agriculture	0.54	0.36	0.43	0.50
2. Mining and Quarrying	0.79	1.00	0.35	0.60
3. Manufacturing	0.53	0.43	0.29	0.25
4. Construction	1.00	1.00	—	0.60
5. Transport and communicatin	0.67	0.63	0.56	0.55
6. Electricity gas, etc.	0.63	0.69	0.37	0.50
7. Other services	0.99	0.82	1.00	0.53
8. Total	0.53	0.39	0.39	0.38

Source: Planning Commission, Government of India Ninth Five Year Plan, 1997-2002, New Delhi, p. 201.

Examining figures in the Table 3.12, there is found the share of manufacturing in the total public and private sector employed declined from 40.0 per cent in 1992 to 34.0 per cent in 1996 and 23 per cent in 1999. The share of plantation and forestry also declined from 7.26 per cent in 1991 to 4.93 per cent in 1999. On the other hand, the share of community and services increased from 33.88 per cent to 4.88 per cent in 1999. The share of transport and communication also increased by about three percentage points during 1981-99.

Role of NSS National Sample Survey Organisation (NSSO) regarding employment in Unemployment situations in the country.

In fact, NSSO provides various features of employment unemployment considerations in the entire economy. The considerations were taken on the basis of nation-wide inquiries that approached towards categories activities such as usual status (US),

Current Weekly Status (CWS) and Current Daily Status. For US, the references period is 365 days. For CWS, it is 7 days and for CDS it is each of the 7 days, preceding the date of survey in each of these cases.

The activity status is determined as working (employed), or not working but seeking work (Unemployed), or not working and also not seeking work the activity status is which a person spends a major part of the 365 days preceding the date of survey is considered his Principal Usual Status (PUS). The activity status in which a person spends a minor part of the 365 days preceding the date of survey is considered as subsidiary usual status (SUS) (NSSO, pp. 5-9).

To elaborate, the person is considered to be employed (or unemployed) on the PUS basis of he was working (or was not working but was seeking work) for a major part of the reference year preceding the date of the survey. The person is considered to be employed (or unemployed) on the CWS basis if he was working even for one hour but was seeking work during the reference week. The employment (Unemployment) on the CDS basis refers to the total person—days of employment (Unemployment) in all persons in the labour force during the reference week (NSSO, pp. 5-9).

Under categorized activity, the organisation conducted survey in different rounds that have made implication of activity for different periods based on rural and urban sectors since 1972-2000, considering economic status (defined). The following table 3.23 number of persons engaged in the activity.

The figures mentioned in the above Table 3.13 that employment rate remained stagnant during the period, 1972-73 to 1987-88 to 1993-94 but there showed declined again during the period 1993-94 to 1999-2000. But the employment rate among males was found substantially higher (6 to 10 percentage points) than females in all areas during all periods. Similarly, there approached higher percentage of activities among both males and females in rural areas than urban areas.

But, we are mainly interested with the resultant of employment rate to persons for mentioned period. Because there existed variation in classified categories of activity to both sexes in rural and urban areas. So to estimate this rate the following Table 3.14 showed unemployment rate since 1972-2000.

Table 3.12
Distribution of Employment in Public and Private Sector in India by Major Industries and Services (Percentage)

Industry	1981	1986	1991	1992	1993	1994	1995	1996	1997	1998	1999
1. Agriculture hunting etc.	7.29	7.06	7.26	7.29	7.24	6.96	6.93	6.79	5.11	5.09	4.93
2. Mining and Quarrying	3.52	3.48	3.27	3.25	3.19	3.24	3.25	3.18	3.56	3.64	3.60
3. Manuf acturing	35.58	35.29	34.5	39.68	33.73	33.78	33.71	34.13	24.43	24.32	23.1
4. Electricity, gas and water	2.44	2.49	2.63	2.64	2.65	2.66	2.65	2.68	3.53	3.54	3.56
5. Construction	4.0	3.81	3.49	3.49	3.45	3.31	3.32	3.29	4.21	4.20	4.19
6. Wholesale and retail trade	2.25	2.25	2.35	2.29	2.3	2.31	2.32	2.27	1.70	1.72	1.72
7. Transport, storage and commu-nicatin	9.15	8.64	8.28	8.31	8.25	8.28	8.34	8.30	11.17	11.18	11.12
8. Finance, Insurance, real estate	3.74	4.41	4.79	4.85	5.0	5.05	5.11	5.09	5.72	5.78	5.88
9. Community, Social and Personal service	32.01	32.56	33.88	33.9	34.13	34.36	34.36	34.24	40.33	40.52	40.8

Note: Employment in agriculture relates to plantation and forestry.
Source: (i) Reserve Bank of India, Report on Currency and Finance, 1995-96, p. 20 and 1996-97.
(ii) Government of India, Economic Survey, 2000-01, pp. S-52 and S-53.

Table 3.13
Number of Persons Employed per 1000 persons according to activity status during the period 1972-73 to 1999-2000

States	1972-73	1977-78	1983	1987-88	1993-94	1999-00
1. US (PUS+SUS)						
Rural area	N.A.	444	445	434	444	417
Urban Area	N.A.	341	340	337	347	337
Total (all India)	N.A.	393	393	386	396	377
2. CWS						
Rural area	378	375	369	362	398	381
Urban areas	367	341	340	354	362	341
Total (all India)	307	307	305	305	325	318
3. CDS						
Rural area	342	341	337	333	361	349
Urban area	292	290	289	293	309	300
Total (all India)	329	315	314	323	335	320

Notes: N.A. = Not–available; the figures for All India are not directly available in the NSSO mentioned above.

Soure: NSSO, Employment and Unemployment in India, 1999-2000, key results, Dec., 2000, pp. 14-15.

Table 3.14
Number of Persons Unemployed per 1000 in the Labour Force in India, 1972-73 to 1999-2000

Status	1972-73	1977-78	1983	1987-88	1993-94	1999-00
1. US (PUS + SUS)						
Rural area	8	16	10	21	11	13
Urban area	54	89	50	57	51	51
Total (all India)	52	52	30	39	31	32
2. CWS						
Rural areas	42	38	40	43	30	38
Urban areas	76	90	71	79	65	64
Totals (all India)	59	64	55	61	47	51
3. CDS						
Rural area	90	81	82	56	56	71
Urban area	108	119	101	104	85	83
Total (all India)	99	100	91	80	70	77

Source: Compiled on the basis of Table 3.13.

Referring the Eights Five Year there might be stated wide variations in the Unemployment rate among different States/Union Territories (UTs) in 1987-88 (Planning Commission, 1992, p. 119 and p. 135). This inter-state disparity persisted in 1999-00 also. There were found variations accounted for their were found variations accounted for there fluctuations in entire geographical areas ignoring the concept of States/UTs. The figures explained that the proportion (PUP) for different States/UTs followed as:

Gujarat	4	
		As per us during 1999-2000
Goa	53	
Arunachal Pradesh	4	
		As per CWS during 1999-2000
Goa	67	
Arunachal	5	
Pandichery	75	As per CDS during 1999-2000
Goa	67	

The high-unemployment-states/UTs (those with a PUP that is higher the respective National average) as per all the three approaches were West Bengal, Tamil Nadu, Orissa, Maharashtra, Kerala, Goa, and Assam in 1999-2000. Similarly, the low-employment states/UTs (Those with a PUP lower than the National average) were Arunachal Pradesh, Gujarat, Haryana, Jammu & Kashmir, Karnataka, Madhya Pradesh, Meghalaya, Mizoram, Punjab, Rajasthan, Tripura and Uttar Pradesh in 1999-2000 (NSSO, pp. 31-36).

Thus, we find that employment and unemployed rate have significantly varied across the States/UTs in India is all the years, including the 1990s. Some of the major high employment-states have been West Bengal, Tamil Nadu, Orissa, Maharashtra, Kerala and Assam.

The employment rate for rural areas and for males was higher than that for urban areas and females, respectively during the 1990s, as in the earlier years. The trends towards an increase in the proportion of casual labour, and a decrease in the proportions of self-employed in the labour force, observed since 1983, continued unabated during the 1990s also. Similarly the trends towards a decline in the share of primary sector employment and an increase in the share of tertiary sector employment, observed since 1983, continued during the 1990s also. The share of secondary sector employment has remained static on the years.

Further, there may be explained that in the post-1950 period, the unemployment rate has been quite high, and on an average it significantly increased during all the decades, including the 1990s, in many industrialized market economics. The young, unskilled and less educated labourers, in particular, have been victims of the high incidence of unemployment in those economics. The high unemployment has engendered the problems of lower living standards, greater income inequality, and greater poverty which in turn, have threatened social cohesion and peace in virtually all the industrial economics. Moreover, in examining proportion of employment and unemployment growth rate by consideration of two decades in the organised sectors of the country following:

Growth rate (%)	1983-84	1994-2000
Employment	2.04	0.98
Organised Sector Employment	1.20	0.53
(a) Public	1.52	0.45
(b) Private	– 0.03	1.87

Source: Compiled from NSSO data (Previously done).

There was found that organised sector employment has not improved in spite of various policy incentives through different Plan exercises, globalization and economic liberalization. Growth of informal sector has been primarily on account of necessity. Therefore to what extent employment generation through normal growth process, where economic growth in terms of GDP is attempted took place or can take place is a subject of debate. If Unemployment is considered a major issue, then the question is whether we should have employment objective rather growth objective in our national Plan.

Also, growth in the organised sector, particularly of small size, is hindered by problems–pressure, unskilledness, ill-motivation to employees. These are the factors accounted for risk investment to the entrepreneurs of the enterprise.

In conclusion, the organized sector's employment came down to near zero and has been negative in most cases, in the public sector. Therefore there requires positive steps to generate employment consideration to the entire areas of the country.

Reflection on Modern Industrial Relation in India

There has been mentioned that employment in the organised manufacturing sector in India remained virtually stagnant since 1980s but the process of major economic reforms was initiated in the country in 1991 and there brought an economic reforms relating to employment opportunity. A study of modern industrial relation in our country can be made in three distinct phases. The first phase can be considered to have commenced from about the middle of the nineteenth century where a series of legislative measures were adopted during latter half of the nineteenth country which can be considered as the beginning of industrial relation in India.

The close of the first world war gave a now twist to the labour policy, as it created certain social, economic and political conditions which raised new hopes among the full of new social order. The constitutional development in India led to the election of representatives in the central and provincial legislative for taking initiative role concerned with social legislature based in International labour organisation (1919) usually meant for greatly influenced the labour legislature and industrial relation policy in India. The second phase related the policy after the first world war followed a number of laws enacted for implementing their policies which where brought during the period of first phase particularly emphasizing on new spurt to the lobour filled to maintained adequate contented labour force for maximising production.

In this context, the government of India taken several steps for evolving measures conducive to industrial peace (1942) making an indication of (a) promotion of uniformity in labour legislation, (b) laying down of a procedure for the settlement of industrial disputes; and (c) discussion of all matters of industrial disputes between employers and employees amounting the conditions of successions made by various governments and representative of employers and workers. These tripartite bodies were essentially deliberative, recommendatory and advisory in nature and the area of their operation depended on the desecration of central government. The states such as Maharastra, (formerly Mumbai). Madhya Pradesh, Uttar Pradesh, Rajasthan and Gujrat enacted their own legislation which were provocative within their states boundaries along with the central legislation.

The third phase was considered as Industrial Force Revolution (1947) at a tripartite conference making an indication of invitation to the labour and management. To assist the government to secure, promote and guaranteed such agreement between the parties and well-wisher in a period of contented and orderly advancement towards a co-operative common wealth. Because it has been observed that the post-independence period of industrial relation policy and at the establishment of peace in industry, and grant of a fair deal to workers through appropriate labour legislation, labour administration and industrial adjudication. State intervention in industrial relation where justified on the ground that it helped to check the growth of industrial unrest and brought for the working class a measure of advance and sense of security based on the principal of industrial democracy at appropriate stages giving for adequate attention to root causes of industrial unrest. Such approaches was brought in the first five year plan (1951 - 56) relating to the problem for requirement of the well-being of working class in the achievement of economic progress that also created an economic organisation in the country based on industrial relation not the matter between employer and employees alone. Further more, it emphasised on necessary changes in the existing laws and trade unions renewing the progress of industrial relations in the country during 1970's for which clarification of mandays in the industrial sector indicated statistical approaches for timeless (in million mandays) in the following table 3.15 since 1971 - 2002

Table 3.13

Years	*Timeless (in million days)*
1971	16.5
1972	20.5
1973	20.6
1974	40.3
1975	21.9
1976	12.7
1977	25.3
1978	28.3
1979	48.9
1980	52.3
1990	61.2
1991	63.2

1992	58.2
1993	52.4
1994	56.3
1995	60.1
1996	62.8
1997	63.9
1998	65.2
1999	66.8
2000	68.1

Source: Planning commission, government of India, 8th & 9th Five Plan, upto 1998, p. 404.

Thus, the genesis of industrial relations in India showed that the state started with a laises-faire policy. And followed it up with protective labour legislation and paternal administration actively interfered in the field of industrial relations treating it as a law and order problems, and subsequently extended its control over almost the entire labour field with greater extended forms.

Explanation of Five Year Plan in venture of employment problems

Explaining over five year plan in India there has been observed that the first five year plan was rather modest in its size and did not take much cognizance of the employment problem as unemployment problem in the country did not exist lie serious forms. With this end in view the total outlay in the first plan was the increase in 1953 by Rs. 180 crores" for financing new specified schemes that simultaneously expanded employment potential and checked growing unemployment in the country. The first plan period stressed the need (a) to make maximum use of idle labour land (b) for increasing employment at rising lands of real income. It was, however, recognised that in an under developed economy elimination of unemployment or even containing at with reasonable limits was, by its very nature a some what long-term process and called for a steady and well directed effort.

Besides, the first plan did open some fresh avenues of employment but on the whole it did not amount to much since the very approach of the plan was modest and theoretically not employment oriented. "The employment situation, as revealed by employment exchange statistics began to show an uneasy trend by the time the first five year plan was half way through. There has, however, been increasing realisation that if plans of economic development are to evoke sufficient response, employment must be one of the eternal objective. It is therefore, a matter of common agreement that the second five year plan should have a better employment opportunity".

Stressing on the problem of unemployment in the second five year plan that second to presume the problem of unemployment linked with the problem of capital investment. To the planning commission". The question of increasing employment opportunities could not be viewed separately from the programmes on investment envisaged in the plan. Because employment in implicit and follows investment, and it is, of course a major consideration in determining the pattern of investment. The main emphasis of given plan was on the problem of industrialisation this plan laid stress much larger expenditure was contemplated on transport and heavy industries which have in the short term a relatively small employment content. The plan tried to bring about a healthy compromise between the capital goods industries on one hand and village and small-scale industries on the other, partly for creating the capital base and partly for solving the unemployment problem.

Following aspects undertaken in case of employment features may be focussed in identification of economic reforms concerned with employment features such as:

(i) Full employment could be achieved only in the longness and with special attention to the plan project.

(ii) For the selection of labour intensive technique several considerations, besides employment, were to be taken into account.

(iii) Although the surplus generated per person in labour intensive technique may be less than per unit of output for capital formation would be greater in the former specially when the total cost of a maintaining the unemployed population were taken into account. Hence the balance of advantage was in favour of labour-intensive technique in an undeveloped economy. Where unemployment doles were not practicable.

Also, the second plan also recognised that expansion of employment opportunities had to be an integral part of the plan and the pattern of investment had to be influenced by it, where employment prospective was found better but not set out the goals unequivocally, because of a significant departure from capital-intensive projects and from the earlier approach to unemployment eradication. This may be attributed to the fact that much of this development expenditure was incurred on heavy industries. Where employment opportunities were not enough in the immediate future.

The third five year plan envisaged the strategy of utilization of mannual labour the construction project, imparting of suitable slectls, fuller utilisation of small scale industrialisation, rural electrification etc. as writnessed below:

(i) The shift in the occupational distribution, already started during the second plan period, shall be carried forward. A perspective assessment for a fifteen year (1961-75) period. Provided that the proportion of work force dependent in agriculture would be reduced to be percent by 1976. This presumed that two thirds of the increase in labour force during the 15 years was to be absorbed outside agriculture.

(ii) Longer gain of employment shall be obtained from the development programmes under taken for this purpose, the unemployment problems was to be divided into smaller units for purpose of isolating the problem areas for concerted attention and use of local resources.

(iii) For an effective utilisation of rural manpower of the plan recommended the implementation of supplementary works projects. A fairly larger number of entrants to the labour force are born in families of self-employed because self-employment in India is predominant as against age employment and this particularly so in agriculture. But, however, the off seasons respond employment opportunity in provisional ways to the persons attached in agricultural and other works.

Thus, the employment features in the third plan period might be taken into account of perspective feature of employment growth assuming that the trend would be continued in future also. About two-thirds of increase in labour force next fifteen years was absorbed outside agriculture, it should be possible to reduce the proportion of the working force dependent on agriculture to around 60 percent by 1976.

However, it is said that the greater weakness of India's third plan was its failure to solve unemployment problem and following objectives have been stressed in fourth five year plan. In considering the expansion of employment over the fourth plan, attention shall have to be paid not only to the new investment but also to a more effective utilisation of existing productive capacities. A major objective of economic and industrial policy should be to sustain current employment at the highest level feasible when substantial development has already been taken place in the economy.

If a plan is to meet the test laid down in (iii) above, it must endeavour to make the most effective use of manpower resources. This implies a fighting out the source of underemployment both in rural and urban areas.

The fifth plan was of the view that the importance of providing adequate and increasing employment opportunities in our development programmes could properly be emphasised. "The basic objective of any development plan must always be the provision of an adequate living standard for all people in the country. More achievement of an increased average per capital income cannot by itself help in the achievement of this objective unless there is a reasonable assurance of being gainfully employed. In a manner, which will not only give remuneration but also social satisfaction in the use of his talents and capabilities. To the extent that any plan falls short of generating adequate employment opportunities, it will necessarily give rise to a degree of social unrest which, if allowed to grow to unmanageable proportions, could wreak the other benefits that the plan may seek to provide.

The fifth plan recognised that the objective of the income redistribution was meaningless unless it was combined with the creation of employment opportunities. In the Draft fifth plan, it was emphasis, at that "Redistributive growth is a major objective of the fifth five year plan. In this context the conventional fiscal measures for redistribution on income cannot, by themselves, make a significant impact on the problem. Since a major cause of inequality is larger scale unemployment and underemployment, the most effective way to deal with it is to provide vastly expanded employment opportunities at reasonable income levels."

The sixth five year plan has been framed to be specific, to some extent, towards the problem of unemployment. "One of the principal objective of the sixth five year plan (1980-85) is the progressive reduction of unemployment in the country."

The above figures of the backlog of unemployment indicate only the long period unemployment and do not take into account the seasonal unemployment and part-time underemployment. The sixth plan has estimated that the present rate of growth of employment to the organised sector can absorb only 4 to 5 million regular additional jobs in the public sector in the course of the plan period. Thus this would still leave large number for absorption in agricultural, small scale sectors and other unorganised activities.

Table 3.16

Backlog of Unemployment, 1990 and net Additions to labour force 1990 - 98

Age group	Backlog 1990	Net Addition 1990 – 98	Total
5*	14.03	43.41	57.44
15*	13.56	42.16	55.72
15-59	14.13	40.72	54.85

Rural female Category is not strictly comparable due to change in the coverage of certain marginal workers.

Source: Sixth five year plan, Govt. of India, Planning commission.

Employment Generation in Different Plans

It is evident from the review of the employment policy adopted in the five year plans, the planning commission has been more and more cautious about unemployment problem in her successive plans. As a result, the succeeding plans provided for larger and larger employment by the expansion of the different sectors in the economy. The Total employment generated in the plans periods, on the face of it, is really a remarkable achievement, but seeing the growing and over increasing size of unemployed army the growth of employment has not been adequate. The growth of employment during the plan periods seems to the more pitiful if it is seen in relation to the growth of output and investment in the economy.

Table 3.17

Project Growth of Employment 1990-91 to 1997-98

	Employment 1990-91	*1997-98*	*Increase*	*Annual Growth of Employment %*	*Annual Growth of value added %*	*Annual Growth of gross output %*
	(Million persons)					
	1	*2*	3	4	5	6
1. Agricultural & activities. etc.	95.561	97.921	2.360	4.41	4.63	6.29
2. Mining and Quarrying	0.998	1.234	0.236	5.36	12.32	12.23
3. Manufacturing	27.867	29.671	1.804	5.23	7.61	8.53
4. Construction	12.596	14.523	1.927	5.123	6.09	8.12
5. Other (Including Service)	52.139	54.693	2.554	6.12	6.52	7.41
Total	189.161	198.042	8.881	———	———	———

Source: Eight Five Year Plan and Ninth Five Year Plan, Government of India Planning Commission, 1998, p. 209.

Further, to follow the growth rate of employment and gross value added at (constant prices). The following table13 shows are extended and expanded organised forms of employment opportunity in different industries of the country.

Table 3.18

Overall Employment in The Organised Sector Number of Persons Employed in Million

End of March Year	Public Sector				Private Sector	Grand Total
	Central Govt.	State Govt.	Quasi Govt.	Total		
1961	2.09	3.01	0.77	7.05	5.04	12.09
1962	2.19	3.09	0.88	7.42	5.16	12.58
1963	2.33	3.20	1.00	7.95	5.45	13.40
1964	2.43	3.43	1.10	8.45	5.78	14.23
1965	2.59	3.59	1.21	8.96	6.04	16.00
1966	2.64	3.72	1.32	9.38	6.81	16.19
1967	2.69	3.77	1.40	9.63	6.68	16.31
1968	2.72	3.80	1.48	9.80	6.52	16.32
1969	2.71	3.90	1.66	10.10	6.53	16.63
1970	2.73	4.00	1.79	10.37	6.70	17.07
1971	2.77	4.15	1.93	10.73	6.76	17.49
1972	2.85	4.36	2.18	11.31	6.77	18.08
1973	2.91	4.57	2.49	11.88	6.94	19.28
1974	2.94	4.71	2.91	12.91	6.79	19.28
1975	2.99	4.75	3.19	1287	6.80	19.67
1976	3.06	4.94	3.39	13.36	6.84	20.20
1977	3.08	5.11	3.68	13.85	6.87	20.72
1978	3.09	5.40	3.91	14.40	7.05	21.45
1979	3.17	5.64	4.14	14.98	7.20	22.18
1980	——	——	——	15.08	7.23	22.31
1981	——	——	——	15.48	7.30	22.88
1991	3.31	5.81	5.41	14.23	8.29	22.52

1992	3.32	5.87	5.62	14.81	8.67	23.48
1993	3.33	5.91	5.79	14.95	8.93	23.88
1994	3.41	5.93	5.79	15.13	9.14	24.27
1995	3.42	5.96	5.92	15.30	9.37	24.67
1996	3.45	5.97	6.22	15.64	9.68	25.32
1997	3.49	6.01	6.29	15.79	9.97	25.76
1998	3.50	6.07	6.38	15.95	10.12	26.07
1999	3.53	6.10	6.48	15.85	10.27	26.52
2000	3.58	6.45	6.79	15.95	10.67	27.48

Including Local Bodies

Sources : 1. Eastern Economist, Annual Number, 1998, p.65.

2. Economic Survey, Government of India, 1994-95.

3. Economic Survey, Government of India, 1998-99, pp. 114-15.

Table 3.19

Growth Rates in Employment and Gross Value Added : Two Digits Industries

(*Percent per annum*)

Industry Code Rate	*Employment Growth Rate*		*Real Gross Value Added Growth rate*		
	1980 - 90	*1990 - 97*	*1980 - 90*	*1990- 97*	*1999-00*
20-21	-1.58	2.70	12.03	7.39	4.41
22	3.71	2.95	08.48	7.83	4.46
23	-3.17	0.58	02.63	0.26	0.22
24	3.02	2.67	13.79	8.35	5.37
25	-3.00	1.06	-4.24	6.56	6.21
26	5.62	11.37	14.63	10.44	8.42
27	-1.79	1.80	5.71	-6.74	6.74
28	0.45	2.30	5.54	3.54	2.88
29	5.91	2.24	11.67	10.46	10.12
30	106	5.22	10.03	9.83	8.85

31	3.73	4.72	14.31	5.82	5.65
32	2.03	0.30	11.54	4.29	3.86
33	0.73	0.91	6.55	11.15	10.10
34	1.58	2.83	3.06	9.98	8.88
35+36+39	3.54	2.56	8.62	7.21	7.11
37	-0.18	2.10	7.13	9.39	10.15
38	2.81	7.14	11.96	18.98	22.26
Manu-facturing	0.53	2.69	8.67	7.43	7.12

Note: Two industry codes:

Source : Compilation based on National Sample Survey Organisation, Annual Report since 1980-2002.

20-21 food products; 22 beverages; tobacco :23 cotton textile; 24 wool, silk, manmade fibre textile;25 jute and other textile; 26 textile products; 27 wood and wood products; 28 paper and paper products; 29 leather and products;30 chemical and chemical products; 31 rubber, plastic and petroleum products;32 non-metallic mineral products; 33 basic metals and alloys;34 metal products and parts; 35-36 machinery and equipment's; 37 transport equipment's; 38 other manufacturing industries; and 39 repair of capital goods.

For given table, a comparison in made between the period 1980-81 to 1990-91 and 1990-91 to 1997-98. It is seen that the growth rate of employment increased in the 1990s in most industries due to reason of favouring common factors in case of large number of industries.

Also the table provided that that in the 1980s employment declined in two digit industries 20-21 food products; 23 cotton textiles; 25 jute textiles; and 27 wood and wood products. Thus, the comparison between two mentioned periods showed an intense and account for 41 employment in 1980. But in this case the declined trend in employment was arrested and reversed in the period 1990s.

In light of given study, the following table 3.20 showed the distribution of percentage of share in employment in different sectors as placed below.

Table 3.20

Percentage Share in Employment of Different Sectors

Year	*Public*	*Sector*			*Private*	*Grand*
	Central Govt.	*State Govt.*	*Quasi Govt.*	*Total*	*Sector*	*Total*
1961	17.3	24.9	06.4	58.3	41.7	100.0
1966	16.3	23.0	08.1	57.9	42.1	100.0
1974	15.2	24.4	15.1	64.8	35.2	100.0
1975	15.2	14.2	16.2	65.4	34.6	100.0
1976	15.1	24.4	16.8	66.1	33.9	100.0
1977	14.9	24.7	17.7	66.9	32.5	100.0
1978	—	—	—	67.5	32.5	100.0
1990	15.0	26.0	16.7	57.7	42.3	100.0
1991	15.1	26.1	16.1	57.3	42.7	100.0
1992	15.0	26.0	16.1	57.1	42.9	100.0
1993	14.3	26.3	16.3	56.9	43.1	100.0
1994	14.1	26.0	16.0	56.1	43.9	100.0
1995	14.4	26.2	16.2	56.8	43.2	100.0
1996	14.4	26.2	16.3	56.9	43.1	100.0
1997	14.1	26.1	16.1	56.3	43.7	100.0
1998	14.0	26.1	16.1	56.2	43.8	100.0
1999	14.2	26.4	16.4	56.4	43.3	100.0
2000	14.1	26.3	16.0	56.3	43.9	100.0

Note : Data cover all establishments in the public sector and all non-agricultural establishments in the private sector employing 25 or more persons. Private establishments employing 10 to 24. Workers are also covered on a voluntary basis.

Source: Eastern Economist, Annual Kumar, 1998, p. 65.

Table 3.21

Employment Generation on in Plans (In Million Persons)

Plans	*Gap*	*Backlog of Unemployment*	*New Entrants*	*Employment Provided*
First Plan (1951-56)	3.3	9.0	7.0	5.3
Second Plan (1956-6w1)	5.3	11.8	10.0	7.1
Third Plan (1961-66)	7.1	17.0	14.5	9.6
Annul Plan (1966-69)	9.6	14.0	11.0	12.6
Fourth Plan (1969-74)	12.6	32.0	18.0	26.6
Fifth Plan (1974-79)	26.6	44.0	22.0	48.4
Sixth Plan (1980-85)	29.9	47.0	26.3	55.2
Seventh Plan (1985-90)	32.8	49.1	30.8	58.1
Eighth Plan (1990-95)	36.7	49.8	34.7	60.8
Ninth Plan 1995-2000)	40.2	51.8	38.1	63.1

Source : 1. Puttaswamiah, 'Unemployment' in India. Policy for Manpower (1999).

2. India, 1999, Government of India, p. 164.

Table 3.22

Investment And Employment In The Plans

Plans (in Crores)	*Investment (in million persons)*	*Employment generation*
First Plan (1951-52 To 1960-61)	4641	7.0
Second Plan (1956-57 To 1960-61)	6750	10.0
Third Plan (1961-62 To 1965-66)	10400	14.5
Fourth Plan (1969-70 To 1973-74)	22635	18.0
Fifth Plan (1974-75 To 1978-79)	47561	22.2
Sixth Plan (1980-85)	59675	26.6
Seven Plan (1990-95)	71893	34.3
Ninth plan (195-2000)	79725	39.2

Source: 1. Planning Commission, Government of India.

2. Puttaswamiah, "Unemployment in India, Policy for Man power (1997)

3. India, 1998, Government of India, p.164.

Further an investment on net national disposable income has been made in consideration of old services (1970-1997) and new service (1993-1999) presented in the following table.

Table 3.23

At Current Prices *Rs. Crore*

	NN Pmp	*Other current transfers From rest of the world*	*Net national disposable income*
Old Service			
1970-71	39958	123	40081
1971-72	42726	163	42889
1972-73	47042	154	47196

1973-74	57415	192	57607
1974-75	67486	274	67760
1975-76	72183	528	72711
1976-77	77881	739	78620
1977-78	88465	1022	89487
1978-79	95608	1042	96650
1979-80	104238	1624	105862
1980-81	124271	2257	126528
1981-82	145341	2221	147562
1982-83	160612	2527	163139
1983-84	187416	2774	190190
1984-85	207828	3101	210929
1985-86	234577	2821	237398
1986-87	261321	2976	264297
1987-88	297241	3499	300740
1988-89	352365	3841	356206
1989-90	405444	3798	479505
1990-91	475794	3711	479505
1991-92	543643	9382	553025
1992-93	621169	8089	629258
1993-94	716854	11276	728130
1994-95	855070	18823	873893
1995-96	993894	221112	1016006
1996-97	1135947	41120	1177067
New Series			
1993-94	763787	16514	780301
1994-95	898802	25416	924218
1995-96	1051289	22112	1073401
1996-97	1214225	43968	1258193
1997-98	1351916	43764	1395680
1998-99	1581753	43241	1624994

Source: National Income statistics, centre for monitoring Indian economy December 2000 p. 18.

Factors Responsible for slow Rate of Employment Growth

It is, therefore necessary to examine the factors contributing to this state of disproportion between the rate of growth of employment and that of investment and output.

The factors responsible for it were enumerated in the First Plan as follows.

(a) The rapid growth of population;

(b) The disappearance of the old rural industries which provided part time employment to a large number of persons in the rural areas.

(c) Inadequate development of non-agricultural sector from the point of view of employment.

(d) The large displacement of population as a result of partition.

The problem has been seriously aggravated in recent year. This is caused mainly due to obvious fact that the development process through the successive plans has been able to create the sufficient employment has not proceeded at a rate proportionate to the growth of industrial output and investment.

They are following:

(i) Decline in employment output and employment investment ration.
(ii) Emphasis on capital intensive projects.
(iii) Change in the structure of output.
(iv) Excessive use of foreign technology.
(v) The wide wage gap.
(vi) Absence of a National Policy.

References

1. Government of India (1956), Planning Commision, Second Five Year Plan.

2. Government of India (GOI) (1977), Report of Review or Pilot Intensive Rural Employment Project, Controller of Publication, Delhi

3. Government of India (GOI) (1970), Report of the Committee of Experts on Unemployment Estimates, Government of India, New Delhi.

4. Government of India (GOI) (1079), Planning Commission Draft-Sixth Five Year Plan 1978-83 (Revised), Government of India, New Delhi.

5. Visaria, P (1980): Poverty and Unemployment; An Analysis of Recent Evidence; World Bank Staff working paper No. 417, Washington, D.C. October

6. Krishnamurty, J (1988): 'Unemployment of India' in T.N. Srivasan and Parnab K. Bardhan (eds), Rural Poverty in South Asia (Bombay, 1988) 298-300.

7. Satish Jha (1986): 'Moonshine On Employment", Economic and Political Weekly, January 25, 1986, pp. 150-52.

8. Hazaria, B and J. Krishnamurty (1970): "Employment Implications of India's Industrialisation. Analysis on Input-Output Framework", Review of Economics and Statistics, Vol. 52, 1970.

9. Government of India, Planning Commission, The Fourth Five Year Plan, 1969-74 (Delhi, 1969), p.15.

10. Suresh D. Tendulkar (1974): 'Draft Fifth Five Year Plan and Removal of Poverty, Economic and Political Weekly, Annual Number, 1974, p. 289.

11. Government of India: Planning Commission, Sixth Five Year Plan, 1980-85, pp. 239-40.

12. Michael P. Todaro, Economic Development in the Third World (New York, 1981), p. 311.

4

Objective of the Study

It is true that employment in organised manufcturing sector in India was stagnant during the 1980s, but few in the 1990s. But after 1990, there has become slow down in the growth in real wages. The period 1990-91 to 1997-98 witnessed that the growth rate of employment in organised manufacturing was 2.69 per cent per annum, well above the growth rate achieved in the 1980s and higher than the growth rate of the labour force.

In 1991, there has been marked an accelerated growth rate of employment opportunity due to irritation of organised manufacturing industries in our country. This growth has been made due to various factors such as; economic reforms, greater market flexibility, increased trade orientation leading to change in the structure of industries following improved access to foreign technology and imported capital goods.

In this context, Ghose (1994) remarked that there created adoption of advanced technology that provided more capital intensive technologies or contracted out increasing volumes of work of smaller enterprises. This increased volume showed a regulated form of job security to the people of the country in the organised sectors in determination of increase in capital intensity attributing the rise in real labour to macro economic policies and labour market conditions.

The implementation of employment programme might be summed up as follows:

(i) Under sections 2m (i) and 2m (ii) of the factories Act, 1948, the industrial unit employed 10 or more workers with power or 20 or more workers without power on any day of the preceeding 12 months are covered.

(ii) In 1976, the Industrial Disputes Act was changed to make it necessary for enterprises employing 300 or more workers to seek government permission to effect lay-offs, retrenchments and closures. This was made applicable to establishments employing 100 or more workers.

(iii) The change in the size structure which occurred in the 1980s should have led to an increase in employment, but this was neutralised by several fctors including a marked fall in employment in cotton textiles and food products industries, which according to Popla (1994) was caused by closure of factories due to sickness and rationalisation to overcome obsolescence.

In India, 90 per cent of the workers are found in the unorganised sector, for which they get no social security benefit, particularly in case of industrial sectors. In fact, in terms of numbers, agricultural workers dominate the total workforce. But this force shows unemployment insurance and other elements of social wage.

Also, in our country, the unemployment rate is 5 per cent but poverty is more than 30 percent that caused inadequate productive and remumerative employment opportunity to the people. The casual labour works also cause in cretion of unemployment situation in the country. Bcause this factore shows a hurdle in existing employment opportunity to the people.

Further, there can be pointed out that insecurity of income is also a characteristic feature of many types of employment, as causal labourers are found in domination to the working field whether organised or unorganised sectors.

There can also remarked that self employment and part time employment do not have share in total employment, as many other countries of the world provide greater opportunities to employment consideration by adoption of these two resources.

The 'labour market' is also a factor that tends to access to employment opportunity. But this access is determined by participation of people based on educational and skill levels of labour market in unorganized sector that may make an amount of total employment in the informal sectors. Also, in our country, these lacks social background due to which there rise employment opportunity to persons who seek employment. The other factors, gender bias in education and other human development shows discrimination of participation of working process. Because occupational structure does not validate on attribute of participation of work exercised by males and females in equivalent manner. In addition to, migration rural-urban is used for enterance of work participation that gives low rate of employment opportunity to the persons.

To have concentration on stated facts, an attempt has been made to give analytical study relating to labour process accounted for employment consideration.

The prime objective of the study is to provide an account of industrial relations that attribute employment opportunity in expanded and intensed forms. Though other countries of the world passed through different stages of development depending upon social, economic and political situation that prevailed in every country in inseparable manner. But the problem arises that how far there existed characteristic of industrial process attributing employment opportunities in India when persons were involved or will involve in the industrial works.

In this context the new economic policy in India enunciated by the Government policy since the middle 1991 there has been existing serious implications for employment consideration qualitatively and quantitatively formations.

However, an argument can be justified for India that can afford the situation where safety and protection of the workers engaged in different industries. It might have been analysed with the working capacity, efficiency and productivity of industrial outputs in case of skilled and non-skilled employment engaged in different instrument of labour force. While labour force has been counted as improved skilled training and experience gained in production contributing towards Industrial produces followed by given opportunity of employment to non-engaged persons.

Now-a-days division of labour has attained greater complexities where some people / workers are found responsible for the managing factories with an application of productivity of various goods.

Undoubtedly, it has been observed that the remaining people have no access to any kind of means of production and also they have no alternative measures but to sell labour power in determination of employment opportunities under socialist set-up. Thus there can't arise the situation of the means of the production being used wholly benefitted to any particular group or the whole population of the country as a whole.

Therefore, the distribution of income and wealth varying conditions are to be examined with adequacy in the present study.

In relation to stated facts, it is obvious that a large number of the countries of the world are found to set-up social organizations based on capital relations of production in form of economic system. Therefore, India is also existing to face the problem of such economic system relating to industrial process contributing to the development of Indian human society accepting the distinctive features between capitalism and productivity where the latter attributes employment opportunities without any discrimination of age, sex and education etc. These factors are found based on laise-fair.

Finding an insight in capitalism there has been found successful to bring about tremendous increase in the productivity for consideration of social labour problem attributing employment opportunities indicating physical and technical bases in form of large scaled industries followed by extended competitions in various forms of capitalism.

But in characterizing labour power as a commodity for our country where skilness, manpower are used to overcome the problems of industrial phenomenon of the country though workers are mercilessly exploited under capitalism in almost all areas of the world.

In observation, the industrial sectors provide high proficiency in asserting employment opportunity to individuals of the population based on distinguished trades, income, patterns of works, skilledness of workers & other factors accorded to existing situations between employers and employees. These are ingredients that are to be performed extensively for completion of the entire investigation of the present study.

In context of stated facts two important guidelines emerge for project industrial units planning and implementation at the national level.

(i) capacity utilisation is for more important than new investment if recession is to be averted; and

(ii) existing source resources should be allotted to these unfinished projects which satisfy the two criteria of early maturation and high income generation so that there may exist widened form of employment opportunity to the individuals of the population.

The guidelines of above criteria make an indication of the form of reforming to a predetermined schedule and taking corrective action when necessary. The predetermined schedule of operation would be the result of a detailed analysis of the aspects of industrial units, using as far as possible the modern technique of evaluation and budgeting.

In examining the industry level, there is growing inclination on the part of the government to involve private industry in the task of project planning and investment. It is towards this end that new measures like price control investment directives to institutional. investors reorientation of industrial development and regulation act, speedy license disposal selective credit assistance and relaxation of production controls have been aimed at.

However, the type of investment will depend on the nature of each industry, more specifically on the standing of individual units in that industry. Hence, the guidelines for project planning at the industry level would not be at the same as at the national level. The present study guidelines would be;

(a) analysis of existing markets and products with a view to identify the most profitable opportunities. This search would not be at the national level but most of necessity extend to the bigger task i.e. 'employment opportunity'.

(b) analysis of the cost involved and the return of investment. This would involve accounting for inflation, a consideration of the new norms being formulated for credit assistance, new methods for investment analysis and capital rationing and grater attention to the management of working capital, and

(c) industrial projects for improved capacity utilisation should be preferred to new projects of short gestation periods should be performed to projects with long gestation periods.

It is to be noted that the method of implementation of industrial project once it is selected is essentially the same as for large development project.

It is the combination of public investments and private investments along mutually accepted lines that will give the necessary fillip to industry and hence to the economy. The list of industrial units must be maintained in order of importance following effective planning and implementation in consideration of employment opportunity either the future growth or depression of the economy.

In view of providing an intuition on industrial patterns for different planning periods, a justifications might be laid that in modern industrial system of Indian manufacturers that had world-wide based markets. Specifying different commodities such as cotton, textile machinery and technology that spread over other countries of the world before the first world war by finding heavy reliance on this textile industry in India. Though India was also dependent of foreign countries for dye-stuffs and other chemicals needed in the cotton textile for making an excellent progress in the world.

Though, India proved deficient during the twenties in case of leasing the opportunities for production, final counts of cotton and manufacture of bleached dyed and printing goods that occur in after first world war.

Further, a concentration could be made on steel product manufactured by TISCO located in Bihar state for carrying out greater extensions in productivity accorded with different programme insued by the same management i.e. TISCO.

Again, it would be discussed on segment ventures provided by Indian Merchants and Entrepreneurs to run steem-ships for the case of shipping, comparison during the First World War. But the growth of Indian Shipping and Ship Building Enterprises particularly meant to run over the management for needed loyalty.

The facts involved in the case of growth of Coal Industry in India from 1930 to 1944, they took place by first and starts, not by plan policy for the industry as a whole or by any conscious choice of investment over a long period. Under the individual where industrialisation process might be counted in exact forms.

Further, an investigation would be made on economic development consisting of natural resources, capital formation, human resources (contributing employment opportunities) marketable surplus of industrial goods, conditions imposed by abroad and economic system that would be dealt analytically. There is no doubt that mass participation in development programme is a pre-condition for accelerating the growth process existing in our country where people show interest in the development activity benefiting mass organisation as social organisations. The growth process participated by people of the country elites the groups to appropriate to the benefit of the growth the general mass of the developed people for their apathy towards state development programmes. Under the circumstances it is futile to hope that masses will participate in development project undertaken by the state that are to be essentially studied for our country. Therefore, the focus would be given on the period of development planning subject to constraints of growth of monopolies in industries concerned with economic power in the modern sector without any disputed fact. Though, most people think that these facts are sufficient to prove that Indian's social organisation is any thing but just. Hence, it is not at all surprising that there is wide spread apathy towards development planning in the country.

Further, the technical know-how and general education directing on the case of development indicating the scientific technological knowledge advances for production of steady rise the productivity level but contributing employment opportunities in number of persons under assumption of linear homogeneous production function and a neutral technical change effecting the rate substitution between capital and labour as explained by (T.N. Shultzin 1961 and A.K. Sen in 1996.)

In light of giving an explanation on wide spread employment that makes an indication of high rate of population growth as enumerated in different censuses of India where it seemed striking symptom of employment in adequate form of development in India. Because there were 22 million unemployed people as against 3.3 million unemployed in 1951 referred by Reserve Bank of India Bullen, 1969.

It is true that the govt. did not provide any data in actual sense of observation that may be believed in meaningful estimation of unemployment. Though lately the planning commission has provided on estimates of unemployment in year 1995 and also the estimates of usual status of unemployment provided by national sample survey in year 1995 and pointed the age group class, 13.89 million people who were unemployed as against 12.02 million in 1990. Such comment of unemployment conditions has been supported by 6th plan period of the country because the nature of unemployment is different from that of the developed country. Most of the unemployment in the developed country of the west is cyclical. During the depression phase of the business cycle, effective demand in these countries show a tendency to decline rendering large number of people unemployed. The same situation as pointed by A.M.

Khenroo in year 1962 that followed the question of unemployment in alarming rate particularly stressing on the problem of urban unemployment in India assuming two forms: (1) the failure of the industrial sector to grow and fast enough rate to absorb the growing urban population and (2) expansion of general education creating unending demand for white collar jobs.

In addition to examine all mentioned facts for industrial process contributing employment opportunities in India, there would be examined 'scarcity of capital' that can alone help a country unlike India in its attempt to overcome its economic backwardness. Because low capital formation proportion means low rate of growth of national product unless capital output ratio declines more i.e. output can be turned out per unit of capital (Simon Kuznetes: 70, 1959).

However, according to preliminary estimates of the C.I.O., rates of gross domestic savings and gross domestic capital formation in 1995-96 were 22.8 and 24.6 per cent respectively. Such rates of capital formation are generally considered enough to realise a reasonably high rate of growth but surprisingly in this country, it has not been possible.

Though, the rate of capital formation has remain consistently high in the recent years, the rate of growth remains stuck at low level. This fact has raised serious doubts about the CSO's estimates of capital formation. Some economists believe that capital output ratio has been more unfavourable than that was assumed to be by the planner. Without doubting the CSO's estimates they assert that the Lewis model of development has become inoperative in India. In other words, they argue that nearly by raising the rate of capital accumulation growth rate can not be pushed up.

Hence, mentioning different objectives for given subject, there is a need for the labour bureaucracy and labour judiciary to develop a human attitude/approval through specialist cadres and continuing educational inputs that may perceive both the socio-cultural and business imperatives in present rapid change of the world.

Further, on the basis of surveys carried out by the National Sample Survey Organisation (NSSO) on a quinquennial basis, some special tabulations of 1993-94 round of survey were obtained to help analyse the employment situation for the prepration of the Ninth Plan. Because the study relating to the employment situation presents a detailed analysis in presentation of Ninth Five Year Plan. Largely based on NSS data, as shown in the following tables 4.1 & 4.2 comprising 'rates of growth of employment and labour force' 'unemployment rates' and unemployment rates in rural and urban areas respectively.

The unemployment rates which have been measured by three different methods of measuring employment, unemployment, i.e., the usual status basis (US), the current weekly status basis (CWS) and the current daily status (CDS) basis. These measures provided the study of three different measures males, females and their total for all rounds of NSSO round to rural and urban sectors in the following Table 4.1

Table 4.1
Distribution of Employment to Male and Females on the Basis of Regular and Salaried Considerations to Rural and Urban Sectors

Rounds		*Rural*	
	M	F	T
32nd			7.7
38th	10.3	2.8	7.5
43rd	10.0	3.7	7.7
50th	8.3	2.8	6.4
55th	8.8	3.1	6.7
		Urban	
32nd			41.8
38th	43.7	25.8	40.0
43rd	43.7	27.5	40.3
50th	42.1	28.6	39.4
55th	41.7	33.3	40.1

Source: NSSO, 2001.

The figures presented the employment solution for both sexes based on 5 rounds of NSS data that have made on implication of employment determination to the country. This study has given clear concept relating to employment situation to both rural and urban areas of the country.

They showed more employability to males than females in both rural and urban sectors. That means to say that the employment opportunity to males followed by increased trend than females to both sectors for all investigation conducted by 5 rounds of NSSO.

Again, we have considered classified employment opportunities to persons/employees for sex rounds of NSSO. The classified employment into UPPS (Unemployed persons sought service), CWS (Current weekly status), and CDS (Current daily status) approached unemployment rate for assigned rounds based on NSSO information's to males and females to sector rural and urban. There is found that unemployment rate among males for all classified employment followed less amount in rural areas than urban areas. Similar situation amongst females when rural and urban sectors were undertaken there.

Table 4.2

Distribution of Unemployment Rate Across Different Categories to Males Females in Rural and Urban Sectors

Rounds	Unemployment rate					
	Male			Female		
	UPSS	CWS	CDS	UPSS	CWS	CDS
			Rural			
27th	—	3.0	6.8	—	5.5	11.2
32nd	2.2	3.6	7.1	5.5	4.1	9.2
38th	2.1	3.7	7.5	1.4	4.3	9.0
43rd	2.8	4.2	4.6	3.5	4.4	6.7
50th	2.0	3.1	5.6	1.3	2.9	5.6
55th	2.1	3.9	7.2	1.5	3.7	7.0
			Urban			
27th	—	6.0	8.0	—	9.2	13.7
32nd	6.5	7.1	9.4	7.8	10.9	14.5
38th	5.9	6.7	9.2	6.9	7.5	11.0
43rd	6.1	6.6	8.8	8.5	9.2	12.0
50th	5.4	5.2	6.7	8.3	7.5	10.4
55th	4.8	5.6	7.3	7.1	7.3	9.4

Source: NSSO, 2001

Note: UPSS-Umemployed Persons Sought Service

CWS-Current Weekly Status

CDS-Current Daily Status

This study revealed the person days unemployment rates in urban areas have been consistently higher than in the rural areas. Though the person days unemployment rate (CDS) has shown a decline over the years, the decline is sharper in the rural areas than in the urban areas. The reasons for this may be that the rural areas provide more opportunities of self-employment.

In addition to various objects as discussed above, the specific object of the study is to give light on a continuous process to ensure the development of employee emphasizing their competencies, dynamism, motivation and effectiveness that ought to explained in exploration of planned process. The continuous planned process (Rao, 1999) by which employees are helped to (i) acquire or sharpen capabilities required to perform various functions associated with their present or expected future roles; (b) develop their general capabilities as individuals and discover and exploit their own inner potentials for their own and organizational purposes; and (iii) develop an organization culture in which superior-subordiate relationships, team work and collaboration among sub-units are strong and contribute to the professional well-being, motivation and pride of employees"[1]

In this context, Maginson viewed in utilization of workforce in the industrial sectors as "the total knowledge, skills, creative abilities and beliefs of the individual involved"[2]

The other concerned auther Dayal (1991) explained capabilities by the following expressions.

(a) ways to better adjust the individual to his job and the environment,

(b) the greatest involvement of an employee in various aspects of his work; and

(c) the greatest concern for enhancing the capabilities of the individual[3].

In dealing with consideration of exercised performance of employee in industrial unit, the system of work must be perspective that may provide learning process to other employees. The process of works in units must follow in classified form depending upon the component of the system of the unit.

Such work process must be followed principles and concepts of behavioural science for the development in promoted and implemented plans that are to be laid on continuous process. The sub-system of continuous process is highly interlinked with social, cultural, economic and political factors-all these factors show significance for relevance to the "quality of human life improvement" is mainly concerned to the quality of work in the industrial units.

These characteristics are to be observed finding an interlinked relation between an industrial units since independence of the country.

In this regard, the main activities of employees have been recognized by distinguished boards concerned with occupational safety and safety of employees that are to be conducted for need-based and specialized training programmes for all types of industries in creation of awareness of safety to employees of the industrial units. Such conduct is provided on specified problems to encourage creative thinking at the gross root level under the frame of policies enacted by international agencies like I.L.O, W.H.O and the British Safety Council, etc.

The Council has so far set up chapters in the states of Andhra Pradesh Karnataka, Kerala, Madhya Pradesh, Maharahtra, Orissa, Rajasthan, Tamil Nadu and West Bengal.

In appraisal of welfare services, the following studies are to be examined with respect to welfare services, labour recommendation by National Commission, social security specifying the conditions of India, workmen's compensation, employees' state insurance, the employee's provident funds and miscellaneous, the maternity benefit, and industrial disputes etc have been discussed in brief to the present study. In addition drawbacks on social security employees to the industrial units to our country has also been traced out for analyzing facts in the entire study of the given subject.

1. One of the main obstacles in the effective enforcement of the welfare provisions of the Factories Act has been the quantitative and qualitative inadequacy of the inspection staff. Besides increasing the number of factory inspectors it is also necessary to improve their quality. They should be specialists in different areas such as industrial hygiene, industrial medicine, etc.

2. At present, a labour welfre officer is not able to enforce laws independently because he has to work under the pressure of management. It is therefore, suggested that he should be appointed by the Government and should work under the administrative

control of the government though the factory to which he is attached may be made to bear his salary.

3. At many places crèches and canteens do not follow the prescribed standards. Women workers do not make use of the crèche facilities either because they are dissuaded by the management to bring their children with them or because they have to face transport difficulties. The National Commission on Labour has made the following recommendations to improve crèche facilities: (a) The Government itself should undertake to provide this facility. It may later on recover a part of its expenditure from employers concerned. (b) The Government should enforce the prescribed standards more strictly. (c) Community crèches near the residential areas should be started so that the working mothers are able to utilize this facility to the maximum extent possible. The National Commission on Labour recommendations for improving the canteen services are as follows:

(a) Workers should be encouraged to run canteens on co-operative lines.

(b) Workers should be allowed to make credit purchases from canteens.

(c) Employers should grant subsidies to canteens in the form of free accommodation, fuel and light, utensils and furniture.

(d) At present a canteen needs to be provided only by a factory employing 250 or more workers. This number should be reduced to 200 workers.

(e) Establishments which operate over a wide area should run mobilecanteens.

4. It is very distressing to note that despite the existence of comprehensive legal provisions the incidence rate of fatal injuries per 1,000 workers in our country has been rising year after year. It was 0.1 in 1984 and 0.26 in 1991[2]. This is several times higher than the rates prevailing in many developed countries such as Japan (0.02), U.K. (0.03), and U.S.A. The worst offenders are the States of Maharashatra, West Bengal, Gujarat, Madhya Pradesh, Tamil Nadu, Rajasthan and Punjab, Together they account for 86 per cent of all accidents.

Five industrial sectors, namely, textiles, metallurgy, machinery manufacturing, chemicals and transport, have been identified as more accident prone accounting for 80 per cent of injuries as per survey conducted by the Industrial Toxicology Research Centre recently. In the textile industry which has 24% of the total employment force, 54% of the industrial accidents take place

Chemicals, fertilizers and pharmaceutical industries pose another big risk to the lives of the workers. It is estimated that some 10,000 chemicals are used by about 4,000 units of the chemical industry in our country. Many times accidents occur due to the improper storage and handling of potentially hazardous substances.

From a study of several accident reports prepared by the Central Labour institute and the Directorate General of Factory Advice Service, Bombay, it is unsafe acts rather than unsafe conditions genrally account for majority of accidents.

The reporting of accidents is done by the first-line supervisor. He sends information to the labour officer who in turn completes the prescribed from for onward transmission to the Chief Inspector of Factories. The chief Inspector generally works under the administrative control of the Labour Commissioner in each State. His duty is to ensure enforcement of statutory provisions in respect of safety, health and welfare of employees. Inspectorates of India are in most cases ill-equipped and inadequately staffed. The number of factories under the charge of an Inspector varies between 150 and 950. The Inspectors are further loaded with various additional duties under the Factories Act. The inevitable result of this heavy load of work is that a very large number of factories are not visited even once a year and, where inspected, the quality of inspection remains doubtful.

Most of the factories do not have any well-defined safety policy. Acequate line support is also not available in many cases. There are no full-time safety officers and the safety functions are looked after by the labour welfare officer or the managers themselves. In the majority of industries safety committees do not exist and safety education is scanty and intermittent. As regards the workers' organizations, they take hardly any interest in accident prevention.

National Commission on Labour Recommendations:

These are as follows:

1. The statutory provisions on safety are adequate for the time being. Effective enforcement is the current need.

2. Every fatal accident should thoroughly be enquired into and given wide publicity among workers.

3. Employers should play a more concerted role in safety and accident prevention programme and in arousing safety conciousness.

4. Safety should become a habit with the employers and workers instead of remaining a mere ritual as at present.

5. Unions should take at least as much interest in safety promotion as they take in claims for higher wages.

6. Every factory employing 100 or more workers should set up safety committees to ensure continued participation of workers in matters connected with safety.

7. Safety officer should be appointed in all factories employing 1,000 or more workers of where the manufacturing process carried on exposes the workers to serious risks of bodily injury, poisoning or diseases (The Factories Act, 1948 now contains this provision vide Sec, 40 (B).

8. The factory inspectorate should advise and assist employers in drawing up induction and training programmes in safety.

9. Industrial safety should be included as a subject in the syllabl of all technical institutions, particularly the industrial training institutes.

10. A standing committee consisting of users of machines, manufacturers and safety experts should be set up for encouraging the incorporation of built in safety devices in new machinery and equipment.

11. Workers' reluctance to use safety equipment (either because it is inconvenlent or because it has been used by others) should be removed through education.

A National Seminar on Safety Management in Industry was held in 1984. Two new recommendations make by this Seminar are:

(a) The licence fee for egistration of factories under the Factories Act should be suitably increased to create additional revenue for strengthening the factory inspectorates;

(b) Safety performance and policy of a company should find place in its annual reports circulated to the shareholders.

Social Security

The connotation of the term "Social security" varies from country to country with different political ideologies. In socialist countries, the avowed goal is complete protection to every citizen from the cradle to the grave. In other nations with less regimented economies, a measure of protection is afforded to all the needy citizens by means of schemes, evolved by democratic processes consistent with resources of the State. According to the Social Security (Minimum Standards) Convention (No 102) adopted by the ILO in 1952, following are the nine components of social security:

(i) Medical care,

(ii) Sickness benefit,

(iii) Unemployment benefit,

(iv) Old-age benefit,

(v) Employment injury benefit,

(vi) Family benefit,

(vii) Maternity benefit,

(viii) Invalidity benefit, and

(ix) Survivor's benefit

Social security schemes may be of 2 types:

(a) Social assistance, under which the State finances the entire cost of the facilities and benefits provided. Here benefits are paid after testing the financial position of the beneficiary.

(b) Social insurance, under which the State organizes the facilities financed by contributions from both the workers and employers, with or without a subsidy from the State. Here, benefits are paid on the basis of the contribution record of the beneficiary without testing his means.

Social Security in India

At present both types of social security schemes are in vogue in our country. Among the social assistance schemes old age assistance schemes are the most important. The government of Uttar Pradesh introduced old age assistance scheme in 1957. This scheme was designed to pay a monthly benefit to needy individuals over the age of 70 years who had no one to support them. Similar schemes were started in Andhra Pradesh in 1961, Tamil Nadu in 1962, Punjab and Haryana in 1963 and subsequently in many other States. However, different States have different eligibility conditions and provide different levels of benefits.

Under the centrally-sponsored National Social Assistance Programme (NSAP) three types of benefits are given to the people who are below the poverty line. These are old age pension, maternity benefit and support on the death of the bread winner. Under the Old Age Pension scheme each person of the age of 65 or above gets Rs. 75 p.m. Under the Maternity Benefit scheme a woman gets Rs. 300 per pregnancy up to the first two live births. Under the third scheme a bereaved family is given Rs. 5000 in case of natural death of its bread winner and Rs. 10,000 in case of death by accident.

The social insurance method, which has gained much wider acceptance than the social assistance method, consists of the following enactments.

1. The workmen's Compensation Act, 1923,
2. The employees' Sstate Insurance Act, 1948,
3. The employees' Provident Funds and Miscellaneous provisions Act, 1952,
4. The maternity Benefit Act, 1961 (described above)
5. The payment of Gratuity Act, 1972 and
6. The Industrial Disputes Act, 1947.

A brief description of the social insurance provision in these Acts is as under:

Remarks

It is consisting of various securities to employees of the industries. It components of medical cane, sickness benefit unemployment benefit, old age benefit, employment injury benefit, family benefit, maternity benefit invalidity benefit and survival benefit have been measured to make implementation in almost all industrial units. Though these components are found varying from country to country with different ideologies. They are followed to the industrial units in democratic process. The benefits are undertaken in terms of financial assistance on the basis of the contribution records maintained by the management of the enterprise. Such benefit has been adopted by the ILO in 1952.

Further, there would be thrown light on workmen's componsation Act, 1923 that makes coverage in several factories, mines, plantation, transport undertakings, construction works, railways, ships, circus and other hazardous occupations specified in Scheduled II of the Act. It does not apply to members of the Armed Forces, Casual workers and workers covered by the Employees State Insurance Act, 1948. The Act is empowered in relation different types of benefits varying from one industrial unit to another in terms of financial assistance followed by the decision of endorsed commissions. The amount of compensation to be paid to a workman depends on:

(i) the nature of the injury caused by accident

(ii) the monthly wages of the workmen concerned, and

(iii) the relevant factor as specified in schedule IV of workman's compensation Act, 1923.

Though, the compensation in terms of financial assistance exists in variation accorded to the nature of appointment to permanent employees. The compensation under the Act is payable by the employer.

These problems have been undertaken to the present study for analyzing factsin consideration of facilities to employees to the industrial units.

In light of compensationto employees to the industrial units, an Act 1948 comprising Employees State Insurance that covers benefits (medical benefit) that reaches benefit to employees in the form of out patient treatment or as inpatient treatment in a hospital which may either be run by the Employees' state Insurance (ESI), Act 1948 corporation or by the State Government.

In such circumstances, the insured person when he is sick, is also entitled to get sickness benefit at the standard benefit rate (specified in Rule 54 of the Employees) corresponding to his average daily wage.

In addition to the Act 1948 also provides different types of benefits such as maternity, disablement dependent and funeral have been taken and adopted to employees' benefits to the industrial units for giving every sort of facility to them subject to the following conditions.

(a) When a person is entitled to any of stated benefits provided in mentioned Act, he shall not e entitled to receive any similar benefit under any other enactment.

(b) An ensured person shall not be entitled to receive for the same period.

(i) both sickness benefit and maternity benefit; or

(ii) both sickness benefit and temporary disablement; or

(iii) both maternity benefit and temporary disablement benefit.

Further, the Act, 1952 emphasised on Employees' Provident Fund followed by various benefits such as, superannuation retirement/short service pension. These factors show evidence of attainment of age to employees accounted for length of service rendering eligibility for pension.

Also, disablement, widow, children and orphan persions payable to them by the Employee' Pension Fund Schemes in industrial Units followed by regulated rules to the enterprise. These studies are to be analysed framing in different chapters for knowing facts to the employees in organized enterprises.

Besides different types of benefits followed by different Acts of Industrial Units, the additional Act 1947 shows Industrial Disputes the Act follows 'disputes' comprising strike, lockout, stagnation and no work, etc emerging closure of factories.

Thus, different formation of Acts relating the case between employers and employees have been enacted since Independence of the country provided an established relationship in almost all factories (organized sectors).

The first and the most important drawback of our social security measures is their fragmented character. This has resulted in duplication and overlapping in the provisions of various Acts. All social security provisions need to be integrated in one Act. The study Group on Labour Legislation which was oppointed by the National Commission on Labour also recommended that an integrated and comprehensive statute called the Labour Code should be formed to bring about uniformity in the definitions of basic terms, in the application of procedures and in the accrual of benefits to workers. This will also reduce the number of administrative authorities working at present.

The second drawback is that the burden of various social security benefits, at present, is born predominantly by the employer. Very little contribution is made by the workers or the state. This is against the social security principle.

The third drawback is that our social security benefits at present over the industrial workers only. Workers in the unorganized sectors do not get these benefits.

The fourth and the last drawback is that there is no effective implementation and enforcement of these Acts. Very often employers do not pay the contributions—records are not kept properly, claims are not processed expeditiously and benefits are not paid in time underpaid or not paid at all.

The arrears of contributions to the Employers Provident Fund and Employees State Insurance have mounted up to Rs. 446 crore as on March 31, 1993[7]. Arrears of provident fund dues are Rs. 267 crore and those of ESI dues are Rs. 179 crore. With regard to the ESI dues Rs. 74 crore of the total arrears cannot be recovered for the present due to various reasons, such as, their recovery being disputed in the courts, factories having gone into liquidation, recovery barred by the enactments of the State and Central Governments, factories closed and whereabouts of the employers not known, etc. Hence, there is need for constituting joint ommittees of the representatives of the workers and management at the establishment level to over see the regular remittances of the contributions to the EPF and ESI. Trade unions can also play a useful role by taking up the issue of mounting arrears seriously. Government should set up special courts to settle the existing disputes expeditiously.

References

1. During 1991 maximum number of fatal and non-fatal accidents were reported from the textile industry. The were 60 and 17,437 respectively.

2. These rates are specified in Rule 54 of the Employees' State Insurance Rules, 1950.

3. Retaining allowance means an allowance payable for the time being to an employee during any period in which the establishment is not working for retaining his services

4. The Indian Workers, Sept., 6, 13, 1993.

5. *Ibid.*, 1994.

6. *Ibid.*, 1995.

7. *Ibid.*, 1996.

5

Witnessing of Industrial Sickness Creating Unemployment Conditions

Making concentration on given study, there is found that the decade of nineties has witnesses a large decline in worker population indicating all segments of population. Because in this connection, the years 1993-94 and 1995-2000, have witnessed a considerable decline in the crude worker population ratios (WPRs) to all segments of the population of India, Viz., namely males and females to both rural and urban sectors. Such cause of declining tendencies in WPRs (1999-2000) rebealed a prolonged debate among scholars and policy makers regarding employment and unemployment situations in the country. This study explained to the population of age group 5-24 (Classified into four groups) for sexes of both sectors based on 50th and 55th. Round Surveys on Employment and Unemployment this study has been made very systematically following points change. In this regard, we have constructed a statistical Table 5.1 in consideration of quinquennial surveys conducted by Sundaram, 2001 that has appeared on next page:

The table 5.1 has made an indication of biggest decline in rural women of age groups 15-19 (by 60 points) and 20-24 years (by 47 points). This decline mentions due to increase in student population ratio it means that the growth rate in (a) the number of rural women in the age group (20-24) who continued their education in this age-group and (le) the number of those in the age group (15-19) who were in higher secondary school was higher than that of urban males and females. Such declining tendency has been raised in WPRs in the age-groups, particularly women due to reason of rising student population ratios.

Table 5.1
Distribution of Age-specific Usual Status Worker Population Ratios (upto 24 years)

Age group	Rural males			Rural females			Urban males			Urban females		
change	50th	55th	Points change	50th	55th	Points change	50th	55th	Points change	50th	55th	Points
5–9	11	6	– 5	14	7	– 7	5	3	– 2	5	2	– 3
10–14	138	91	– 47	141	96	– 45	66	49	– 17	45	36	– 9
15–19	577	503	– 74	364	684	– 60	356	314	– 40	123	105	– 18
20–24	859	844	– 15	456	409	– 47	674	658	– 16	180	155	– 25

Source: National Sample Survey Organisations 50th and 55 Round Surveys on Employment and Unemployment

Deregulation of labour Market

This study would reveal with great deal of industrial sickness based on organised sector employment followed by slower GDP, Population, Workforce and labour force. These factors have provided empirical values since 1977-2000 in percentage distribution by considering 11 variables as presented in the following table 5.2.

Table 5.2
Distribution of Rate of Growth, Organised Sector Employment, Labour Force, Workforce and Unemployment (1977-78) to (1999-2000)

Variable	1977-78/ 1983	1983/ 1987-88	1987-88 1993-94	1993-94/ 1999-00
GDP at 1993-94 Prices	3.8	4.1	5.6	6.5
Organised sector (Total)	2.0	1.1	1.0	0.7
Public Sector	2.6	1.5	1.0	0.1
Private Sector	0.6	0.1	1.2	2.2
Population	2.0	2.4	2.1	1.8
Workforce (P + S)	2.1	1.8	2.1	0.8
Labour force (P + S)	2.0	2.0	2.2	0.9
Workforce (P)	2.6	2.0	2.3	1.3
Labour force (P)	1.8	2.2	2.2	1.3
Unemployment in live (register) unemployment	10.3	6.1	3.3	1.9
Estimated from NSSO Data	– 11.8	9.1	– 2.7	1.2

Note: P–Principal, S–Subsidiary

Source: National Survey organisation data from 32nd, 38th, 43rd, 50th and 55th rounds on Employment and unemployment, Visaria (1996); Registrar general (1996), Reserve Bank of India (2000).

The above tables provided slower employment growth than output. Finding gap in 1919's, the slower rate is existing highly peaked than other previous periods. Because, both public and private organised sector greoo slower than output. While the public sector decelerated continuously declined where the private sector drvyotaccelerated in the last two sub-periods. Organized sector employment grew slower than population workforce (usual status principal and subsidiary workers taken together) and labour force. They explained that either unorganised sector or unemployment or probably both may have increased. Data from employment exchanges has shown that unemployment was growth faster than total organised sector, labour force and workforce calculated with and without subsidiary workers in this context, the growth of unemployment derived from the National Sample Survey Organisation (NSSO) data had shown wide fluctuations. However so far as deregulation is concerned the evidence of late 1980 has shown that private organized employment picking up and increasing at a faster rates then workforce and labour force defined broadly.

Reserve Bank defined a sick industrial unit as that unit which incurred a cash loss for one year and in the judgment of the Bank, was likely to continue incurring cash unit that creates imbalance in financial structure to the unit in measure of 1:1 current ratio. This loss in financial structure has shown worsening trend in debt equity ratio i.e. total outside liabilities to the net worth. As against this definition, the term lending institutions defined a sick unit when it hard incurred continuous cash losses for a period of two years or continued erosion in the net worth by 50 per cent; and continuous default in meating four consecutive half yearly installments of interest or principal in respect of institutional loans. But the State Bank of India has defined industrial sickness in terms of failing in generation of internal surplus on continuous basis. The Bank has also mentioned that industrial sickness has performed dependenancy for its survival upon frequent infusion of funds (i.e., its continuous dependence on frequent help of outside funds).

With reference to the enactment of the sick Industrial Companies (Special Provisions) Act, 1985, has now settled the issue. Clause (0) of sub-section (1) of section 3 of this Act defines "Sick industrial Company being a company registered for not less than seven years) which has at the end of any financial year accumulated losses equal to or exceeding its net work and has also suffered cash losses in such financial year and the financial year. The same clause provides that, for the purposes of this clause; (i) "cash loss" means loss as computed without providing for depreciation; (ii) "net worth" is the sum total of the paid-up capital and free reserves; (iii) "free reserve" means all reserves credited out of the profits and share premium account, but does not include reserves credited out of revaluation of assets, write back the depreciation provisions and amalgamation.

Another sick of industrial unit known as "incipienty sick"

has been defined as that if a company which has eroded 50 per cent or more of its peak net worth during any of the preceding financial years.

But the Act, 1985 shows provision for a number of exceptions. For instance, it does include a government company. Even in the case of companies which are not covered by defined Act, those units are not considered which have not been in existence under the provisions of the companies. Act, 1956 for seven years or more. In context of such definition of the act following companies are also not covered under the Act.

1. A financial or leasing company, which does not own one or more industrial undertaking.
2. A trading company, which does not own one or more industrial undertaking.
3. A company, which owns an industrial undertaking, but which does not during the preceding twelve months employ 50 or more persons, if manufacturing process is carried on with the aid of power or 100 or more persons, if manufacturing is carried on without the aid of power.
4. A company which owns a small-scale industrial undertaking or an ancillary industrial undertaking (Chaudhary, 1987).

Further, in order to have concentration on set-back to employment prospects, there may be remarked that an industrial unit will render the workers unemployed. The implication of sickness to industrial units, creates the situation of unemployment. Because a large number or persons are found deprived of employees as observed in cotton textile mill. The avenue of employment to qualified skilled and experienced workers suffer and they are more restricted to have entrance in industrial units for showing their performance in process of productivity to any enterprise of our country. So there arises an acute problem of surplus industrial labourers that causes adverse effect in economy of our country.

Thus, in order to give focus on such burning situation (an un related phase between industrial sickness and employment situation) of our country is to be carried out with deep study following empirical evidences that occurred in our country since her independence.

Relevance of Ancillary Industry

Ancilarisation of sub-contracting occupies a significant position in the industrial sector of our economy. It lies its direct impact on economies of scale and employment generation. The process of ancillarisation involves greater interdependence between large and small industries and fosters the spread of industry and greater employment.

Large units: They are taken into consideration of undertaking the overall assembly of many sophisticated parts and components that are used for constituting the finished products. This is due to the fact that specialisation and technological measures are now considered to be the most important factor for industrial progress. The importance of concillary units make specialisation in the manufacturing of specific components and parts to the prescribed quality standards and specification of the parent units following relationship between the parent unit and the small or ancillary units augmenting industrial productivity. Such augmentation provides better utilisation of the inputs at the national level.

To spread the process of ancillarisation in the industrial sectors of our country stress in encouraging subcontracting emphasizing steps involved in packages for last three decades in our country. This proces explains for investment in plant machinery not exceeding Rs. 45 lakh as against Rs. 35 lakh for the case of small scale industrial units conversing for production of other articles. This creates a guaranteed market for the output of ancillary units. But in the case of large units the provision is made for indirect pressure at the time of licensing or providing long term capital for the large unit within the list of 800 reserved—the production of variety of industrial components and parts manufactured automobiles, electric products to the small sector. In the public sector, the Bureau of Public Enterprise has been encouraging the growth of ancillaries around large undertakings.

Thus, there can be remarked that the growth small scale industries, including ancillaries in India constitute a very important part in the development of industries of the country though little attention has been made towards this issue. In fact, the great strides mad by Japan in the industrial sphere is the result of such kind of interdependence.

This policy shows the attribute of 60 to 70 per cent of small industry's output in considered ancillary to medium and large scale units in our country. Hence, the issue of small scale industry and the process of ancillarisation assume importance for in depth understanding.

Profile and Rates of Unemployment in Case of Industrial Sickness

On the basis of the NSS data the special group has estimated the number of unemployment persons in consideration of employment opportunities. It is true that the growth rate of unemployed persons works out to be 4.74 per cent per annum for the period, 1993-94 to 1999-00, as against a decline in the number of unemployed persons during the period, 1983-94. The special group Report mensions: The present rising unemployment is primarily considered as a declining job creating capacity of growth observed since 1983-94. The employment growth fallen 1.07 per cent per annum is the per cent between 1983 and 1993–94 to 6.7 per cent between 1993-94 and 1999-00 (Planning Commission P. 2).

In consideration of the two factors employment and unemployment in India the following figures in mentioned table 5.3 have shown employment growth rate (per cent per annum), for both rural and urban sectors since 1983 to 2000.

Table 5.3
Distribution of Profile of Employment and Unemployment

	1983	1994-94	1999-00	Employment Growth rate (% per annum) 1983-to 1993-94	1993-94 1999-00
	(Million persons)				
All India					
1. Population	718.20	894.01	1003.97	2.0	1.95
2. Labour force	261.33	335.33	363.33	2.43	1.31
3. Work force	239.57	315.84	336.75		
4. No. of Unemployed (2–3)	21.76	20.13	26.58	– 0.08	4.74
5. Unemployment rate (%) (4/2 × 100)	8.33	5.99	7.32		
Rural					
1. Population	546.61	658.83	727.50	1.79	1.67
2. Labour force	204.18	255.38	270.39	2.15	0.96
3. Work force	187.92	241.04	250.89	2.40	0.67
4. No. of Unemployed	16.26	14.34	19.50	1.19	5.26
5. Unemployment rate (%)	7.96	5.61	7.21		–

Urban					
1. Population	171.59	234.98	276.47	3.04	2.74
2. Labour force	57.15	80.60	92.95	3.33	2.40
3. Work force	51.64	74.80	85.84	3.59	2.32
4. No. of Unem-ployed	5.51	5.80	7.111	0.49	3.45
5. Unemployment rate (%)	9.64	7.19	7.65		

Source: Planning Commission (2002), Report of special group on Targetting ten Millennium Employment opportunities per year.

Further, an investigation has been made for breaking-up of Unemployed to both sectors rural and urban areas following by the Table 5.3.

Table 5.4
Break Up of Unemployed
(Rural Urban 1983-2000)

	1983	1993-94	1999-00
All India	21.76	20.13	26.58
	(100.00)	(100.00)	(100.00)
Rural	6.25	14.33	19.47
	(74.7)	(71.2)	(73.3)
Urban	5.51	5.80	7.11
	(25.3)	(28.8)	(26.7)

Note: Figures in bracket are percentage (All-India) figures
Source: Derived from table 5.3.

Explanation of following Situation of Employment

In context of this study, the special group Report mentions; The employment elasticity of 0.52 during the 1980s and early 1990s. Went down to 0.16 in the late 1990s. This is primarily due to

(a) The present policy of shedding excess labour that this sector (Organised sector's employment generating capacity measured in terms of employment elasticity) is carrying in order to meet the growing market competition, often known as right sizing,

(b) The trend towards increasing capital intensity per unit of output and

(c) The pattern of growth moving in favour of capital intensive sector.

Inter-State Employment Ratio

In view of examining inter-state employment rates, there is found greater regional disparities in 1999-2000 as compared to 1990-94. In the regard, the following table 5.5 has provided Unemployment rate for periods 1993-94 and 1999-2000 to 16 major states of the country as well as India. This study mentioned inter-state employment scenario.

Table 5.5
Inter-State Employment Scenario

State	Unemployment Rate	
	1993-0-94	1999-2000
Kerala	15.51	20.97
West Bengal	10.00	14.90
Tamil Nadu	11.41	11.78
Assam	8.03	8.03
Andhra Pradesh	6.69	8.03
Orissa	7.30	7.34
Bihar	6.34	7.32
Maharashtra	5.09	7.16
Haryana	6.51	4.77
Gujarat	5.70	4.55
Karnataka	4.94	4.57
Madhya Pradesh	8.56	4.45
Uttar Pradesh	3.45	4.08
Punjab	3.10	4.03
Rajasthan	1.31	3.13
Himachal Pradesh	1.80	2.96
All-India	5.99	7.32

Note: Figures are based on the current status. States have been arranged in the descending order of unemployment rates in 1999-2000.

Source: Same as table 5.3.

The Table 5.5 has shown that in 1999-2000, the unemployment rate in Kerala was 20.97 per cent of the labour force and the lowest rate of 2.96 per cent was observed in Himachal Pradesh.

Also, in 1999-2000, the states which show higher unemployment rates than the national average of 7.32 per cent are Kerala (20.97 per cent), West Bengal (150 per cent), Tamil Nadu

(11.78 per cent) and Assam and Andhra (8.03 per cent each). On the other extreme are states which low Employment rates including Uttar Pradesh (4.08 per cent), Punjab (4.03 per cent), Rajasthan (3.13 per cent) and Himachal Pradesh (2.96 per cent).

High Rate of Unemployment Youth

This study reveals high rate of youth. Unemployment mentioning the age group 15-29 years for seven states Kerala, West Bengal, Assam, Orissa, Bihar, Himachal Pradesh and Maharashtra are found highly effected as shown in the following table.

Table 5.6
Distribution Unemployment Rates (15-29 years) to 16 major states as well as India to both Rural and Urban Sectors

State	*Rural*	*Urban*
Kerala	363	343
West Bengal	266	240
Tamil Nadu	181	156
Assam	146	266
Andhra Pradesh	99	148
Orissa	113	255
Bihar	110	244
Maharashtra	104	165
Haryana	81	83
Gujarat	67	85
Karnataka	58	105
Madhya Pradesh	49	146
Uttar Pradesh	61	125
Punjab	70	95
Rajasthan	44	88
Himachal Pradesh	61	205
All-India	110	154

Note: States have been arranged in the same order as that of table 5.3.

The special group, therefore, opines, "This shows that apart from the genuine problem of employment for the rural sector, positive policies are needed to generate employment in the urban sector and especially among the youth, educated and skilled. This is especially needed because the organized activity, which dominates the urban sector is suffering from a near gob less growth.

(Special group report p. 32.)

Measure of Unemployment Rate by Employment Profile of Various Aspects

This study has given reflection on Consumption Classes (lower and upper) are organised and unorganised sectors usually known as public and private sectors followed by employment profile consumption classes.

The employment rate (CDS) to both rural and urban areas provide monthly per capita expenditure (Rs.) For the period 1999-2000 based on NSS survey 55th round (1999-2000) by making classification of Rs. following in the Table 5.7.

Table 5.7
Unemployment Rates by House hold Monthly Per Capita Expenditure Class (1999-2000) Percentage of Labour Force

Monthly per capita Expenditure (Rs.)	*Unemployment Rate (C D S)*	*Monthly Per capita Expenditure (Rs)*	*Unemployment rate (CDS)*
Rural		Urban	
0-225	11.31	0-300	9.61
225-255	9.62	300-350	9.67
255-300	8.12	350-425	8.20
300-340	7.46	425-500	9.20
340-380	6.56	500-575	9.20
380-420	6.18	575-665	8.63
420-470	6.48	665-775	8.19
470-525	6.14	775-915	7.19
525-615	5.60	915-1120	6.65
615-775	6.06	1120-1500	5.68
775-950	5.57	1500-1925	4.67
950 above	5.25	1925 & above	4.10
All	7.21	All	7.65

Source: NSS Survey 55th Round (1999-2000)

Note: CDS–Current Daily Status

The figures presented in the above table 5.7 give a significant implication for the population below the poverty line. There is found unemployment rate situation higher in lower consumption classes than in the upper ones, with the former recording a nearly 100 per cent higher unemployment rate than the latter.

Organised Vs. Unorganised Sector Employment

The organised sector is dominate by the public sector with specification of mining electricity and water and community and social services. In order to concentrate on employment generation in the unorganised sector of the economy that includes self employment and small business. Its main employment generations are considered by agriculture and allied activities trade, restaurants and hotels including tourism, some social sectors like education and health small and medium enterprises (SMEs) mainly in the rural non-farm sector and transport and construction.

To examine the employment scenario in India there may be estimated unemployment rate for the period 1983-2000 based on compiled and computed data from the Report of the special group on targeting ten million employment opportunities per 2002. Therefore 9 sector of activities have been undertaken into consideration for determining employment elasticity to the specified periods as shown on next two pages in the tabular form.

Again, an analysis of organised sector (Public and Private sectors) that gives employment scenario to the period 1999-2000 followed by percentage distribution to both public and private sectors. For this study 9 sectors as described previous in table 5.8 have been undertaken into consideration. Table 5.9 has been constructed for the same to estimate unemployment rate.

The figures presented in the table 5.8 and 5.9 showed that the employment in the organised sector has been hardly 8.34 per cent accounting for 5.7 and 2.57 per cent to public and private sectors respectively in the total employment generated during 1999-2000.

However, in the unorganised sector the SMEs provided 80 per cent of the manufacturing employment and there is found a more favourable effect on employment further the another source of employment in case of agriculture there accounted 57 per cent of India's total employment for the same period. The elasticity 0.70 was found high between 1983 and 1993–1994 whereas, the post-reform period (1993-1994, 1999-2000) its employment elasticity has sharply declined that has made greater change. The changes have come in different sectors such as horticulture, floriculture, agro-forestry and water sheds etc.

Table 5.8
Distribution of Employment Scenario since 1983-2000

Sector	Employment (Current daily status) (in million)		Employment growth rate			GDP Employment growth elasticity rate (per cent per annum)			
	1983	1993-94	1993-94 1999-2000	1983-1993-2000	1993-1994-1999-2000	1983-1993-2000	1993 1999-2000	1983-1993-1994	1993 1994- to 1999-2000
1. Agriculture	151.35 (63.18)	190.72 (60.38)	190.94 (56.70)	2.03	0.02	2.9	3.1	0.70	0.01
2. Mining & Quarrying	1.74 (0.73)	2.54 (0.80)	2.26 0.67	3.66	– 1.91	6.2	4.7	0.59	– 0.41
3. Manufacturing	27.69 (11.56)	35.00 (11.08)	40.79 (12.11)	2.28	2.58	6.0	7.8	0.38	0.33
4. Electricity gas and water supply	0.83 (0.34)	1.43 (0.45)	1.15 (0.34)	5.29	-3.55	8.4	6.8	0.63	0.52
5. Construction	7.17 (2.99)	11.02 (3.99)	14.95 (4.44)	4.21	5.21	4.9	6.3	0.86	0.82
6. Trade, hotels and restaurants	18.17 (7.58)	26.88 (8.51)	37.54 (11.15)	3.81	5.72	5.6	9.2	0.68	0.62
7. Transport, storage									

Sector	Employment (Current daily status) (in million)		Employment growth rate		GDP Employment growth elasticity rate (per cent per annum)				
	1983	1993-94	1993-94 1999-2000	1983- 1993- 2000	1993- 1994- 1999- 2000	1983- 1993- 2000	1993 1999- 2000	1983- 1993- 1994	1993 1994- to 1999- 2000
and communications	6.99 (2.92)	9.88 (3.13)	13.65 (4.05)	3.36	5.53	6.1	8.7	0.55	0.63
8. Finance, insurance, real estate any business service	2.10 (0.88)	3.37 (1.07)	4.62 (1.38)	4.54	5.40	10.1	8.4	0.45	0.64
9. Community Social & Personal Series	23.52 (9.92)	34.98 (11.08)	30.84 (9.16)	3.88	–2.08	5.7	8.4	0.68	– 0.25
10. All	239 (100.00)	315.84 (100.00)	336.75 (100.00)	2.70	1.07	5.2	6.7	0.52	0.16

Figures in bracket are percentages of total employment in the respective columns

Source: Compiled and Computed from the Report of the Special Group on Targeting Ten million Employees Opportunities per year (2002)

Table 5.9
Distribution of Employment Scenario (1999-2000) in India

	Total	Organised Sector	Public		% of organised Sector to total Organized Private	% of public sector to Total Employment Total	% of public sector to Organisedtotal sector Employment	% of private sector to organised sector
	1	2	3	4 (2 + 3)	5 = 4/1	6 = 2/1	7 = 2/4	8 = ¾
1. Agriculture	190.94	0.52	0.87	1.39	0.73	0.27	37.16	62.84
2. Mining and Quarrying	2.26	0.93	0.09	1.02	44.69	41.15	91.41	8.59
3. Manufacturing	40.79	1.57	5.18	6.75	16.55	3.95	23.25	76.25
4. Electricity, gas and water supply	1.15	0.96	0.04	1.00	96.96	83.48	95.91	4.09
5. Construction	14.95	1.11	0.07	1.18	7.90	7.42	93.97	6.03
6. Trade, hotels and restaurants	37.54	0.16	0.32	0.49	1.31	0.43	23.54	66.46
7. Transport, storage & Communications	13.65	3.08	0.07	3.15	23.08	22.56	97.81	2.19

(contd.)

	Total	Organised Sector			% of organised Sector to total Organized	% of public sector to Total Employment	% of public sector to Organisedtotal sector Employment	% of private sector to organised sector
			Public		Private	Total		
	1	2	3	4 (2 + 3)	5 = 4/1	6 = 2/1	7 = 2/4	8 = ¾
8. Finance in service, real Estate and business services	4.62	1.30	0.36	1.66	35.71	29.14	78.34	21.66
9. Community Social and Personal services	30.84	9.79	1.70	11.49	37.26	31.74	85.21	14.79
Total	336.75	19.42	8.70	28.11	8.34	5.77	69.06	30.94

Note: Employment (in million) on current daily status basis
Source: Same as for Table 5.8

In context of given study, changes have been brought in the inter and intra-sectoral composition with appropriate labour intensive technology. The same report indicated significant increased weightage sector (health, education etc).

Growing Industrial Sickness Creates Low Employment and Low Employment Elasticity

This study would give reflection on industrial sickness that causes low employment rate i.e. unemployment situation to the people of the country. The study requires a brief comparative structure of employment conditions of both organised and unorganised sectors referring tenth plan period. To have concentration of such specific information's collected data and analysis regarding output and productivity of organised sector (public and private) and unorganised sectors are evolved for two main periods 1993-94 and 1999-2000 as shown in the following Table:

Table 5.10
Distribution of Output and Productivity of Organised and Unorganised Sectors of the Economy

	Organised Sector			*Unorganised*	*Grand*
	Total	*Public*	*Private*	*Sector*	*Total*
	1	2	3	4	5
Value added Gdp (Rs crores at 1993-94 prices)					
1993-94	2,56,849	1,80,843	76.006	4,41,143	6,97,992
	(36.8)	(25.9)	(10.9)	(63.2)	(100.00)
1999-2000	4,18,930	2,66,519	1,52,401	6,00,425	1,009,345
	(41.1)	(26.1)	(15.0)	(58.9)	(100.00)
Growth rate	8.50	6.68	12.30	5.27	6.52
Bank Credit	80.8	28.1	52.7	94.9	175.7
(Rs. 000 crore)	(46.0)	(16.0)	(30.0)	(54.0)	(100.00)
1993-94	80.8	28.1	52.7	94.9	175.7
	(46.0)	(16.0)	(30.0)	(54.0)	(100.00)
1999-02	247.4	66.8	180.6	145.9	393.3
	(62.9)	(17.0)	(45.9)	(37.1)	(100.00)
Growth Rate %	20.5	15.5	22.8	7.4	14.4
Employment (Million) 1993-94	27.18 (8.6)	19.30 (6.1)	19.30 (2.5)	288.6 (91.4)	315.84 (100.00)
1999-02	28.11	19.42	8.69	308.64	336.75

Growth rate %	0.56	0.10	1.64	1.12	1.07
Employment elasticity	0.006	0.015	0.135	0.213	0.165
Labour Productivity % per annum	7.88	6.67	8.38	4.10	5.38
Relative labour Intensity (organised/ unorganised) 1999-2000	0.1345				

Notes: Figures in brackets are percentages of the grand total in the row. 2. Outstanding bank credit refers to all scheduled commercial banks.

Source: Compiled and computed from the planning Commission (2002), Reports of the Social Group on Targeting Ten Million Employment opportunities per year

Analysing figures of the above table 5.10 there was found that in the unorganised sector, the employment elasticity was as high as 0.213 in 1999-2000 whereas in the organised sector it was as low as 0.066 i.e., a gobblers growth. There was also found that in the year 1999-2000, the total contribution to employment by the organised sector was only 8 per cent of which the private sector segment's contribution was hardly 2.5 per cent. The balance 92 per cent came from the unorganised sector. In this context, the special group, therefore opined; On this basis one can see that even if the organised sector grows at the rate of 20 per cent per annum and the private organized sector grows at 30 per cent per annum. Their contribution to the total employment with increase hardly by 1.5 to 2 per cent of the total the Tenth Plan. Further, the Group has remarked that this proposition, however, remains hypothetical since given the capital intensity in their sector of today (above 5.5), this high growth will not be sustainable because of the saving investment constraint of the economy. On the basis of this ground reality the Group conducted that for exclusively generating the desirable high level of employment we have to target the organised sector, including small and medium enterprises, which also covers a large part of the services sector of the economy that makes conduct of future strategy but specifying the Tenth Plan Period.

The figures in presented table 5.10 Revolved that in 1999-2000, the unorganised sector contributed nearly 59 per cent to the GDP, but its contribution of employment was if the order 92 per cent. In addition, its contribution to exports was also substantial. But it was late of such opening up of the economy. Such economy was held due to reason of withdrawn of several key subsidies though the unorganised sector had to face consequences of growing sickness. The other factor during 1993-94 and 1999-2000, the policies of liberalisation became more inclined towards the organised sector from 46.2 per cent in 1993 to 62.9 per cent in 1999-2000, whereas in the unorganised sector from 53.8 per cent in 1993-94 to 37.1 per cent in 1999-2000. The unorganised sector continued employment to 92 per cent of the workforce in the economy though it had to face different conditions involved in policies of liberalisation with reversed resultant.

Following India's economic reforms and WTO rules, the special Group emphasized on important factors to the unorganised sectors as indicated below:

(a) To encourage the use of labour-intensive.
(b) To implement capital-saving technology in general;
(c) To make increase of labour intensity seven times per unit of production to the unorganised sector as compared to the organised sector.

Hence, it is therefore, the unorganised sectors in our country exist more vital and reliable in provision of job to persons of the country. But this is only possible when stress would be given on non-sickness of industrial to unorganised sectors of the country.

However, programmes and policies compatible with India's economic reforms, must give stress on unorganised sectors for finding greater approach to the employment opportunities in the foreseeable future to have the following:

(a) Contribution of employment generation;
(b) Consideration of excess labour;
(c) Continuance off increased level of capital intensity;
(d) Identification of activities concerning agriculture social forestry animal husbandry fishing, horticulture to the related areas indusion with education, technology, trainee health etc.
(e) Decision making in implementation of specific programme based on creating tangitute assets;
(f) Contribution of measure additional jobs for developing important exports to large manufacturing beneficiaries;
(g) Appropriate delivery systems to large scale enterprises with proper attention of administrations.

These are the principal evolved in industrial growth and

employment for co-existing with large industries based on high priority for relation of new environment so that there does not arise the problem of unemployment to the people of the country. But, these factors are only possible when the programmes policies concerning industrial sickness must be stressed by the government or interference of institutions. Because, industrial sickness shows great hindrance of closure of enterprises where does not arise the question of employment opportunities.

Impact of Industrial Sickness on Unemployment

Industrial sickness pertains to provision of adequate avenues for gainful employment which is essential for economic health of a nation, particularly to India. The problem of industrial sickness arises due to various causes such as low-capital-intensity, limited development of medium-sized enterprises and imbalance between consumer goods and capital goods industries.

However, it was only after independence that the government realised the village and small scale industries importance and provided them due place in industrial policies. The objective of the industrial policy are to the village and small scale industries througgh five year plans. As such, the plan outlay of the Government of the SSI increased in the successive plans to consider reduction of incidence of unemployment and to improve economic health of the society. There have been recognised three nature of unemployment. First of these is the Current Daily Status unemployment rate which is a more representative indicator for intensity of the unemployment rate. In addition to the general unemployment problem, two of its faces are much more acute and fraught with serious repercussions namely youth unemployment and unemployment among the educated.

In consideration of these problems concerning unemployment situation in the country, the progress of 1991 new industrial policy resulted in more number of SSI units followed by employment value of production. In this regard the annual compound growth rate (ACGR) shows employment level, value of production and value of exports for the process large scale industries to derive benefits of the scale of economy in all respects.

In the context of given studies the following Tables 5.11 show plan outlay for the development of small scale industries and 5.12 for their growth—employment, production and exports in India since 1985-86 to 1996-97:

Table 5.11
Plan Outlay for the Development of Small Scale Industries in India from 1985-86 to 1996-97

Year	Industrial	Total	2 as percent	2 as per cent of
1985-86	5503	33060	16.6	9.52
1986-87	5620	39149	14.4	10.96
1987-88	5337	42921	12.9	11.14
1988-89	5898	48070	12.3	11.63
1989-90	6665	55530	12.0	12.09
1990-91	6374	58369	10.9	13:77
ACGR 1985-86 to 1990-91	3.81	12.12		
1991-92	6565	64751	10.1	14.33
1992-93	7444	72852	10.2	13.37
1993-94	8481	88080	9.6	13.58
1994-95	9088	98167	8.3	16.64
1995-96	10808	1072380	10.3	16.60
1996-97	12280	129189	9.5	13.58
ACGR 1991-92 to 1996-97	13.13	14.46		

Source: Government of India, Economic Survey 1985-86 to 1997-98, Economic Affairs, Vol. 48, Qr. 2, April-June 2003, p. 79.

Table 5.12
Growth of Small Industrial Units in Terms of Employment Production and Export in India, 1985-86 to 1996-97

Year	*Production at current (Rs. in crores)*	*Employment (in lakhs)*	*Export in (Rs. in crores)*
1985-86	61228	96.00	2769
1986-87	72250	101.40	3643
1987-88	87300	107.00	4372
1988-89	1064000	113.00	6489
1989-90	132320	119.60	7625
1990-91	155340	125.30	9664
ACGR			
1985 to 1990-91	20.99	5.52	28.19
1991-92	178699	129.80	13883
1992-93	209300	134.06	17784
1993-94	241648	139.38	25307

1994-95	296990	146.56	29608
1995-96	356123	152.61	36470
1996-97	412636	160.00	39248
ACGR 1991-92 to 1996-97	18.62	4.33	23.86

Source:
1. Government of India, Economic Survey 1985-86 to 1996-97, Economic Affairs, Vol. 48, Qr, April-June 2003.
2. Dr. G.S. Prasad and Kaushic.
3. Fifty years of Small Scale Industries India, Laghu Udyog Samachar, Jan-Dec. 1997, to p. 27.

The new industrial policy shows an attribute of Survival of the indigenous industries, certain branch of goods to be manufactured by SSI units, competence stiff competition and etc. These combined factors might be summed up in three words: liberalisation, globalisation and privatisation.

But it is emerged that there is rapid decline of population and the growth rate of labour force for the reason of industrial sickness. To examine this hypothesis, an analysis of the employment data collected in the various quinquennial surveys conducted by NSS. In their 27th and 55th rounding is presented in the following Table 5.13.

Table 5.13

Annual Rate of Growth of Population, Labour Force and Employment

Period	*Percentage*		
	Population	*Labour Force (UPSS)*	*Employment (UPSS)*
1972-73 to 1977-78	2.27	2.94	2.73
1977-78 to 1983	2.19	2.04	2.17
1983 to 1987-88	2.14	1.74	1.54
1987-88 to 1993-94	2.1	2.29	2.43
1993-94 to 1999-02	1.93	1.03	0.98

Source: Planning Commission, as cited Economic Survey 2001-02, Government of India, Ministry of Finance, New Delhi.

The figures presented in the above Table 5.13 suggest that

alongwith the decline of population the growth rate of labour force based on Usual Principal and Subsidiary Status (UPSS) has also been continuously declining from 2.94 per cent during 1972-73 to 1977-78 to 1.03 per cent during 1993-94 to 1999-00. However, during the period 1987-88 to 1993-94 the growth rate of the labour force was higher than the previous two quinquennial surveys due to a high growth rate of population in 1970s. The growth rate of employment also followed the same pattern, though they remain less than the growth rates of labour force except for the periods, i.e., 1993-94 to 1999-2000, it even went down to less than one per cent per annum. Thus, economic growth in the post-liberalisation era has not been accompanied by enough employment opportunities for the growing population of the country. This is caused by industrial sickness.

On the other hand, employment in absolute terms has risen from 303 million in 1983 to 374 million in 1993-94, i.e., a rise almost at the rate of 2 per cent per annum. During the last period, i.e., 1993-94 to 1999-2000, it rose at the rate of only 0.98 per annum, while the growth rate of population was a little less than 2 per cent per annum. The deceleration in the growth rate in employment is primarily due to decline labour force. Participation in 1999-2000 as compared to the previous period. Such decline in labour force has been industrial sickness. Though the policymakers, statement and administration make it a point to allocate high percentage of budgetary allocations in the plans to come to develop the industrial enterprise for contributing 40 per cent to the gross turnover of the manufacturing sector, about 45 per cent of the manufacturing exports and 35 per cent of the total export.

Non-recruitment in Case of Industrial Sickness

In fact, an enterprise is found suffered from recruitment of employees when it is laid in industrial sickness. There are no set rules for recruitment, selection and there are no set rules for recruitment selection and development if employees. In industries, employees are selected from known circles to ensure their honesty and loyalty in order to employ skilled and educated persons who are efficient and professional, firms should follow modern management rules for the selection and training of employees for accurate and better results. The selection of an employee can be public or private employment exchanges, trainin institute or newspaper advertisements trade union and trade or professional associations. After selection the recruitment is made familiar with the enterprise, its policies and goals. Before placement, training is imparted by qualified trainers on the job to reorient skills, attitude and expected behaviour to perform the job effectively. In certain businesses, job rotation, specialised training or management development training is also considered necessary.

So when there exists industrial sickness to an enterprise/ industry, the output of an employee does not provide significant result and there is no paramount importance. It is true that productivity is linked to the employee's performance. Though modern management suggests various ways for personnel managers to appraise job performance. The basic objective of such an exercise is to measure an employee's strengths and weaknesses and aim for greater efficiency and improvement. Towards the this end opportunities are provided in order for the employee to improve upon and develop to the required lend of skills. So the industrial sickness disrupts employment opportunities and skillness and efficiency of the employee do not have good approch for job responsibilities.

Thus in case of industrial sickness, there is meant great major deviation from the impression for level of skills, particularly in the newly emerging technologies. The deviation takes place highly inadequate in case of the Indian labour force.

Effect of Industrial Sickness in Recent Decade

The study of unemployment among the educated and technically trained persons the proportion of unemployed per hundred persons was 1.5 per cent and 4.7 per cent in both rural and urban sectors respectively during 1999-2000 according to the UPSS concept of unemployment, where as it was 7.1 per cent and 7.7 per cent according to CDS based concept of unemployment. But this reflects the average level of unemployment in the population. This reflection shows an attribute of direct concern between educational status of person and unemployment of educated labour force. According to the 1999-2000 NSS survey report, as high as 57 per cent of there unemployed in rural areas and 63 per cent of those unemployed in urban areas are educated defined as those possessing secondary level education and above). Similarly, the incidence of unemployment (UPS Concept) among the educated (Secondary and above) is 6.9 per cent and 20.4 per cent among rural males and females as against 2.1 per cent and 1.5 per cent general Unemployment rate (UPS Concept). In urban areas as well as unemployment rates of males and females are 6.6 per cent and

16.3 per cent among those educated upto secondary and above as against 4.8 per cent and 7.1 per cent general unemployment rate. But it needs to be observed that among the educated those who do not possess any vocational skills constitute above 69 per cent of the educated unemployed. Thus indicating the significances of the role of vocational education and training in reducing the incidence of unemployment among the educated. However, even all of those educated and possessing vocational skills are not able to get employed since 31 per cent of educated unemployed are these who do possess professional skills. Measures of the extent of facilities for higher as well as lower level of technical education.

For measuring the extent of facilities for higher as well as for the lower level technical education, two variables have been used, namely.

(a) derivation of composite indices for each state as well as their ranks

(b) coefficient of variation

For these studies, computation has been made since 1995-96 and 2000-01 to obtain composite indices of higher and lower technical education as mentioned in the following tables:

Table 5.14
Statewise Composite Index of Level of Technical Education and Ranks since 1995-2001

State	1995-96		2000-01	
	Index	Rank	Index	Rank
Andhra Pradesh	158.30	4	176.37	4
Assam	35.55	16	28.47	16
Bihar	21.32	17	15.11	17
Gujarat	83.41	9	178.02	3
Haryana	207.60	3	112.39	8
Himachal Pradesh	144.53	6	151.01	5
Jammu and Kashmir	105.10	8	81.07	10
Karnataka	76.40	10	102.65	9
Kerala	354.55	1	353.03	1
Madhya Pradesh	39.92	13	45.19	12
Maharashtra	272.85	2	257.12	2
Orissa	41.99	12	57.67	11
Punjab	153.97	5	124.68	7
Rajasthan	39.64	14	39.24	14

Tamil Nadu	123.47	7	148.81	6
Uttar Pradesh	55.87	11	42.00	13
All India	100.00		100.00	
CV (%)	90.51		88.29	

Source: Source as table from 5.13

Table 5.15
Statewise Composite Index of Higher Level Technical Education and Ranks since 1995-2001

State	*1995-96*		*2000-01*	
	Index	*Rank*	*Index*	*Rank*
Andhra Pradesh	120.42	4	146.62	5
Assam	43.09	13	34.56	14
Bihar	34.74	16	19.00	17
Gujarat	91.58	7	114.45	8
Haryana	92.10	6	145.38	6
Himachal Pradesh	75.90	8	67.05	11
Jammu and Kashmir	46.40	11	50.90	2
Karnataka	286.68	1	231.76	4
Kerala	104.61	5	148.99	10
Madhya Pradesh	46.01	12	61.45	1
Maharashtra	266.13	2	243.84	15
Orissa	28.33	17	33.44	7
Punjab	63.90	9	117.56	16
Rajasthan	36.06	15	30.42	3
Tamil Nadu	225.40	3	230.36	13
Uttar Pradesh	39.32	14	35.38	12
West Bengal	48.36	10	36.65	
All India	100.00		100.00	
CV (%)	80.20		74.74	

Source: Data collected from Publications, Government of India (1995, 2000b 2002c) and Planning Commission (2001 b)

Table 5.16
Statewise Composite Index of Technical Education and Ranks since 1995-2001

State	*1995-96*		*2000-01*	
	Index	*Rank*	*Index*	*Rank*
Andhra Pradesh	119.77	7	133.30	6
Assam	47.79	16	40.64	16

Bihar	25.37	17	24.67	17
Gujarat	104.75	10	150.80	4
Haryana	140.95	4	125.73	7
Himachal Pradesh	105.38	9	113.49	9
Jammu and Kashmir	125.23	6	80.84	10
Karnataka	139.93	5	121.01	8
Kerala	249.26	1	272.13	1
Madhya Pradesh	72.05	11	72.47	11
Maharashtra	248.42	2	231.65	2
Orissa	61.68	12	51.37	12
Punjab	110.64	8	148.10	5
Rajasthan	48.61	15	41.24	15
Tamil Nadu	141.80	3	167.39	3
Uttar Pradesh	52.01	13	43.54	14
West Bengal	50.24	14	46.40	13
All India	100.00		100.00	
CV (%)	62.93		68.38	

Source: Data collected from Publications, Government of India (1995, 2000b 2002c) and Planning Commission (2001 b)

Process of preparing three above table with regard to calculate composite indices, the following steps are undertaken as:

It is obvious that having taken a broad-sweeping view of development of technical education in the countries and specialties of labour market scenario. We turned to examine state level picture in terms of relative levels of attainment in the sphere of technical education and changed in it overtime. For this purpose we have prepared an unweighted composite index; of overall development of technical education facilities but technical education facilities may not be equally developed at the higher and lower levels of technical education. Therefore we have also prepared two separate unweighted indices of technical education, one for the higher and another for the lower level. Higher level technical education incorporated data pertaining to:

(i) Engineering and Technical Colleges, including IITs and IIMs;
(ii) Medical Colleges; and
(iii) Polytechnics

Lower level technical education facilities are taken to include data pertaining to;

(i) Industrial Training Institutes (ITIs), both in private and in the government sectors; and

(ii) Arts and Crafts schools

For measuring the extent of facilities for higher as well as for the lower level technical education, two variables have been used, namely;

(a) aggregate the number of institutions for both levels and

(b) aggregate of involvement for two separate categories of levels of institutions.

Eliminating Process of Industrial Sickness Regarding Unemployment

For the overall economic development of any country unlike India, the quality of human resource is accounted as important factor that ensures optimum utilisation of technology for contributing improvement of national output. The human resources are continued in consideration of generating ideas of starting business, technical in employers and management skills in the management to run the business through a process of trial and error. In this manner, the business is passed on from generation to generation even in the event of failure of the business when there is incidence of industrial sickness linked with "unemployment"; so for elimination of industrial sickness, there are required factors training, incentives, industrial relations and adherence to labour laws for planning, organising, coordinating and controlling an enterprise.

Manpower Planning

To the industrial sector, manpower planning is usually considered as one-man show or a group decision with regard to their responsibilities or those of their employees. In fact there is no assessment of manpower requirements no job analysis, no job description and no job specifications but they are aware of their business policies and of the goals to be achieved for a checking manpower required in case of specific positions and assign specific roles to each employee.

To make utilisation of manpower recruitment, selection and development of employees are counted for ensuring their honesty and loyalty with regard to run business/industries in adequate forms and paramount performances. Because productivity which is always linked with employees performance to channelise their skillness for attaining greater efficiency and improvement in consequence of following labour laws.

In addition employees satisfaction is paramount importance for the continuity of the business activity or running the business in grading jobs; formulating wage seals for each job specification, proposing effective means of stimulating and rewarding employees and providing for stability of employment. These are important factors that share in non-incidence of industrial sickness and their make solutions of elimination of unemployment to persons/ employees.

Employees Motivation

In consideration of such assigned factor motivation at work is the most important requirement; Motivation is conceived with self inspiration, propelling an employee or person into action and keeping him at work. It is psychological concept requiriing the management to look into the forces operating with an individual including his/her safety needs, social needs and ego needs as well as the factors that motivate him/her to act or not to act in particular way. Thus for abstaining industrial sickness a positive balance should be maintained to ensure a continuous and dynamic process for the success of the enterprise in terms of; (a) Higher efficiency; (b) better human relations; (c) lower absenteeism and turnover; and image of the enterprise.

In this connection, Herzberg is two-factor theory of motivation consists of main tenance and motivational factors. It is presumed that Indian management personnel are aware of this theory. Maintenance factors are external to the job feel relate to the job environment and include the policy of the enterprise, supervision, interpersonal relations, working conditions, salary, job security status and personal life. Motivational factors relate to the job itself and include feelings of achievement, recognition, challenges at work advancement, increased responsibility and opportunity for growth. They are uni-directional i.e., their effect can be seen in one direction. Maintenance factors create dissatisfaction whereas motivational factors create satisfaction. Attention should be paid to employees with regard to both factors for higher moral and productivity.

Effective Communication

This is also one of the important factors for abstaining industrial sickness that requires for developing positive attitudes among employees. To any enterprise to be more effective, this factor necessitates effective supervisions, effective staffing, coordination and control as well as industrial harmony and peace. Three-way communication channels—upward, downward and horizontal between departments should be defined as important personal functions. Forms of communications, oral or written, should specified with adequate clarity, flexibility and maximum participation at each level in order to enhance efficiency and productivity in the unit.

Maintenance of Industrial Relations and Labour Laws Legislated by the Government

In fact, no enterprise can survive without worker cooperation and industrial peace. Therefore, efforts should be made to ensure that relations between workers and owners managers of the firm remain peaceful. However, disputes are frequent due to various expectations of both employers as well as employees. The Government has legislated certain basic norms to be followed to avoid dispute and maintain peace so that industrial sickness must be untouched of industrial sickness to the enterprise. Also there may be obtained maximum output from the combined activity in the interest of nation's economy. The legislation can be categorised as:

1. Laws regulating conditions of work in factories and establishment
   - General laws, applicable to all factories and establishment
   - Specific laws, applicable to specific industries like the Mines Act, 1952, the Indian Merchant Shipping Act 1923, and the Plantation Labour Act 1998.
2. Laws relating to specific matters like wages and social security measures.
3. Laws relating to workers association and disputes like the Trade Union Act, 1926 and the Industrial Disputes Act, 1947.
4. Laws relating to children and women workers.
5. Laws relating to social security measures.

The first laws reveals general norms regulating and dealing with working conditions in factories with regards to workers health, employment of young persons, leave, wages and penalties for defaults. The act of second law makes an attribute of wages in consideration of minimum time, minimum price rate, guaranteed time rate and over time rate. The minimum rate of wages is consisted of basic rate and cost of wages is consisted of basic rate and cost of living allowance, basic rate with or without the cost of living allowance and the cash value of the concessions in respect of essential commodities supplied at concessional rate. This law shows considerable factors such as payment of wages to employees specifying spent time to workers to the enterprise. The other remaining laws in form of different acts are of paramount importance describing maintenance of industrial peace and avoidances of employee dissatisfaction. Though it appears to be daunting prospect, this is possible irrespective of the size of business, by ensuring effective two-way communication in the enterprise.

To be effective industrial units, various measures have been indicated in adequate and regular forms. But, the enter friendship is considered under chaotic and stressful conditions. However, for achieving success in implementation of entreneurship, rationalisation of many involved in motivations traits and values are required there. Because persons/employers possess traits and values that are accounted for more successful in the role of entrepeneurs, than those who do not have them. The alienated factors, achievement, power, positive work value, risk taking propensity, internal control orientation, high level of aspiration and preference for participative and natural task (NT) styles of leadership are essentially required to the employees. On the basis of these factors, the agencies for entrepreneurship development programmes, can draw an elaborate programme to identify potential entrepreurs, develop them through a series of proper training courses and to help them run their enterprise successfully.

Besides mentioned factor, there is multi-dimensional activity included with designing structure, control systems, process, practices and rule that are extended in promoting entrepreneurial behaviour. Many established institutions and organisations are inhibiting to bring about economic growth in entrepreneurial orientations for achieving potentiality revealing variables personality traits and psychological characteristics. These are the factors considered for target of mass education awareness. Such awareness shows achievement oriented atmosphere, generally tends to develop high achievement motivation for programmes of entreprenureship.

The remaining factor self employment, particularly to rural

youth has been considered as the part of the effort to uplift the vast majority of rural poor living below the poverty line during the sixth plan period. This programme has been accepted to evaluate the impact of the programme both at the macro and micro levels. Such opportunity has been reached to the planners and development administrators for ensuring livelihood considerations to the poor on a substantial basis. With the launching of the Sixth Five Year Plan (1980-85) various programmes have been initiated making the fulfillment of the government up India's equipment. The commitment has been considered suitably equip rural youths of below poverty line (BPL) families with requisite knowledge, skills and technology with a view to boost returns from the assets and open up new non-traditional economic opportunities to beneficiaries so far tied to low level of production due to numerous socio-economic and constraining factors. At macro level, training under this programme was imported through a network of recognized training institutions and master craft persons, based on guide lines which specified skilled artisans, industrial and servicing units, commercial and business establishments, voluntary organisations etc. could provided the required training.

This factor attributed appreciable extent emerging alliances between the private sector and government. Therefore traning needs to be conceived and promoted in consequence of existing promotion and cooperation.

References

Chatterjee, A (1992) : Ancillarisation : Its Significance and Utility, Yojana, January 15, 1992.

Choudhary, U.K. (1987) : Sick Industrial Cos. Act *The Economic Times,* May 5 and 6, 1987.

Puri, M (1992) : *Indian Industrial Economy,* Himalaya Publishing House, New Delhi.

Government of India, Planning Commission, The Sixth Five Year Plan, 1980-85, p. 260.

Industrial companies (Special Provisions) Act 1985, the Reserve Bank.

Mukerjee, A and K.D. Nayer (1986): Financing Sick Units: Laizez faire Vs State benevolence", *The Economic Times,* October, 25, 1986.

Jhosi, V.K. (1987): '*Management of Industrial Sickness,* Jaipur, pp. 57-59.

6
Restructuring and Characterising the Structural Changes Accompanied With Industrialisation

To the Post-Independence India, the employment structure has been assumed with the concept of modernity by making clarification of region and special spirit of industrialisation in the country that differ from the setting up of the British rule. The approaches in regard to economic development which in the modern context means, approaches of industrialisation have been assumed to understand the degree on underdevelopment. The degree of underdevelopment was ranging since the British colonial period and they did not approach in employment consideration.

In this context, employment has provided the concept of opportunity of participating in the process of growth and making contribution to the growth of industrial wealth. Because it has been undertaken into consideration of self sufficiency and employability that makes an individual for gaining dignity. Though a number of employment concerning the national economy approaches have been deviced for finding development, increase did not unemployment and the following generating volume of working generating in the national economy in light of this aspect of study, the industrialisation process has developed the problems of under employment that characterized a sharing in a situation of productivity to this society. For developing countries unlike India where the problem of employment is found a chronic problem in view of large number of people below poverty line and also not involvement of persons in participation of productive activities. This sort of situation has created a long-term social problem and therefore, the achievement of employability could not be solved neither in the form of traditional employability and modern nor productivity of the developed society.

In this regard different suggestions have been attended for giving an indication of the extent of the industrialisation that is meant for employment in the industrial sector or value added but also something more than that. To over come this difficulty Thomson, Linge and Cant have evolved a composit index based on three mode factors to measure regional concentration. However, Alexander and Alexander and Lindberg are of the opinion that since there exist strong correlation between these alternative of the degree of industrialization for finding significant results. To analyze their result they have indicated for finding correlation co-efficiencies by measuring different indicators as well bull cross section and time wise data but there effort could not approach towards real pattern of self-employment approaches.

Present day is inductive in character and is using industrial employment as a surrogate for measuring the extent of industrialization associated with employment situation of the country. For extent of industrialization, capital or value added to follow surmountable difficulties that make a situation of difficulty in substantial special and temporal variation in the prices of capital goods as well-inputs and outputs.

In realisation of structural changes in industrialisation process, the employment conditions have been obtained with reference to industrial employment (Standing Orders) at, 1956 in various industrial establishments, the conditions have been covered between employers and employees by making understand mutual context for entrance of employee the following conditions have been restructured with reference to mentioned acts.

(a) Classification of workmen, e.g. whether permanent, temporary, apprentices probations or badlis.
(b) Manner of intimating to workmen periods and hours of work, holidays, pay days and wage rates.
(c) Shift working.
(d) Attendance and late coming.
(e) Conditions of procedure in applying for, and the authority which may grant leave and holidays.
(f) Requirement to enter premise by certain codes and liabilities to search.

(g) Closing and reopening of section of the industrial establishment and temporary stoppage of work and the rights and liabilities of the employer and workmen arising there from.
(h) Termination of employment and the notice thereof to be given by employer to workmen.
(i) Disciplinary action in relation to misconduct towards employer constitute different forms of punishment.
(j) Unfair treatment or wrongful exception by the employers are also counted as a matter of unparliamentary governance.

Besides mentioned facts, changes in industrial structures have been brought for following factors service records; conformation; age of retirement; transfer; medical aid in case of accident; medical examination; secrecy an exclusive service.

In order to solve the employment situation of the country different scholars are found directly involved in analysing data based on Census of Moving Industry (C.M.I.) and Annual Survey of the Industries (A.S.I.) since 1945 for finding greater intensity in the industry that is related with employment problems of the country. These datas are found highly related for solving employment situation of the country used for industry labour force of different regions of the country. The region give crude indices of industrialisation for making an interpretation of the employment situation. Though the employment situation may vary with different variables such as wages proportion to value added, value added per worker, average labour cost and, ratio of non- production workers. These factors deal with proportion with adoption of technical changes for developing countries like India. Because the industrial process in our country is completely dependent upon developed technologies in relation to economies that reflect the factor prices.

In order to make specific situation of employment concerned with industrial process we are to make understand the specific relation between size of the industries and its pattern of location because these two terms are mainly related with external economies that are to be concentrated with capital labour issues electricity consumed that may provide indication of the extent of mechanisation that is substitution capital for labour.

In addition to characterized structure of industry there attains proportion of raw material cost in the value of output and the proportion of raw material cost in the total cost of production.

Besides the above factors for restructuring of industrial process, market orientation results more to minimise the transportation cost for supplying the final product. Wherein analysis of a firm tends to move closer to the market in the same proportion as it moves from the raw material orientation. The market orientation of the industry in general can be said to capture the joint effect of the variables transportation cost, supply and product cost, etc. In light of this study a justification may be given that market orientation is one of the important variable for which decision of location of firms demands and analysis of industry wise for castes may be considered for giving emphasis on special concentration of industries to any region. The region for the industrial organisation must parse for adequate number of market accorded to the size of the population, purchasing power capacity, and indication of power capacity income for full fledges industries. This sort of variable expenditures the degree of urbanisation for the industrial sector.

The structural changes brought in industrial process have also been examined with the employment trends between output and employment considerations for growth of industrial output an investment in different plans and periods of the country. For instance, the first plan has stressed to make maximum use of idle labour for increased employment at rising levels of income. This plan has made to eliminate employment situation in extended firm for giving well directed efforts. This plan was also interested in realisation of economic development to evoke sufficient responses through employment considerations of the country.

The second plan laid greater stress on the problem of unemployment and under employment by means of substantial increase of rapid industrialisation emphasising on national income and reduction of income inequalities. This plan has presumed the economy of the country by reducing the unemployment situation and turned towards the increased employment opportunities by making different programmes of investment. The investment in the second plan was meant to achieve employment, labour intensive technique as well as imbalanced proportion for employment and unemployment considerations.

The third plan has been undertaken by the government for imparting of suitable scales fuller utilisation of small scale industry and programmes and rural industrialisation, rural electrification by making adoption of construction approach for absorption of manual labours that also provide an employment opportunities for generating income to the wealth of the society. This plan has created a balance between development on employment under different formulations and adaption of development policies by assigning priorities with potentiality of works for which there has been marched imbalanced in employment opportunities in anticipated employment opportunities.

Analyzing the role of planning in India concerned with employment opportunities to public and private enterprises, it is important to note that mixed economy is inherent as a dominant character in the country. For achieving mixed economy of the country the plans have directed for measure segment of economic life through the endeavor of employment problems. These problems have made regulation and incentive to realize the situation of employment to Indian people. The operational goal of the plans were to achieve an increase in the national income at desired level of investment as well income ratio, and also to reduce inequalities of income and concentration and economic power for generating additional employment opportunity whether by means of casual labour force.

The sixth plan of the country also provides criteria for evaluation, plan experience growth modernization and social justice in view of these criteria. The employment opportunity adheres balance regional development following transformation of measures land reforms and minimum need of programs that have been considered necessary for balanced regional developments different constraints have been imposed by three important postulate, namely, removal of regional balance is not possible in the short run, the long run cannot combined high rate of interest and removal of regional imbalances and the development of infrastructure facilities would follow special spread of industrialization. For acceptance of these post lanse, the planners made their concentration by giving their considerable attention to the inter-sectoral balance rather than that of regional imbalances. Therefore, to translate the regional development policy is to practice several adhoc groups and committees which are appointed for making solutions in identification of regional development of the country. For example, the Pandey Committee was set up to suggest the objective criteria for identifying industrially backward regions as compared to the criteria suggested by the earlier working groups that deal with the over all backwardness. In this context, the Pandey Committee use certain indicator for identifying industrially backward state in purview of criteria evolved particularly, for nine states that is Andhra Pradesh, Assam, Nagaland, Orissa, Rajasthan and Uttar Pradesh and also four Union Territories that is Goa, Himachal Pradesh, Manipur and Tripura. The committee could recognise these states as backward regions and suggested suitable strategy for the industrialisation of backward regions by using capital, interest and tax subsidies at the initial stages of the production.

The recommendation of Pandey and Wanchoo working groups followed the industrially backward states for receiving subsidies under central scheme of investment. These measures have been adopted for backward localities in the industrially developed states linked with employment opportunities to the affected people.

In this way there have been adopted different measures endorsed by different committees for development growth centres accorded to the size of population of the areas.

In recommendation of establishment of different types of industries to the industrial works, there have been identified following rules; wages; provident fund; hours of work and rest intervals leave with wages and allowance compensatory and other allowances; classification by grades provision of new rules or discipline among employees and also nationalisation, standardisation of improvement of plan etc. These constraints have been inacted in different act setting up for authorities indicating different modes such as conciliation enquiry and adjudication for observation of these factors. The process of negotiating team accompanied by personal manager, production manager and company lawyers as well as chairman who looked towards the selection of representatives particularly in case of recruitment.

Besides the stated factor the working conditions of the employees have been analytically studied for finding differences of works among the employees. The differences have been pointed out to heredity and environmental factor. The hereditary factor mainly determine physical traits such as high wage and strength while environmental factor generally have dominant involved on personality traits and interests. In context of these knowledges physical traits have not only been applied rather in mental and social surroundings performance of the recruited persons have been agreed as industrial psychological attempts for finding the affect of workers efficiency. The purpose of knowing mental environment among workers was to know mental strains caused among the worker while at work adversely affect their efficiency that means to say, through the mental environment the employers might know the psychology of workers concern with works as well social environment. The social environment stresses the situation of environment affected on the society.

Thus during the time of recruitment of the workers in industries different factors are found in provision of impacts of industrial safety on productivity in particular case of hazardous industries like chemical and fertilizer. Because safety measures prevents accidents, which are disastrous to both employees as well as employers. The measure of safety has been assumed for showing performance fearlessly and creating confidence among the employees so that productivity might be brought in consistent forms to the initial period and follows upward trend in productivity in the long run.

Implication of these measures, there has been recognized workmen compensation act by indicating the following informations such as number of employees in the unit, severity of the accident, kind of the work or occupation in which the employees are found and engaged in activities and also shift of workers. These factors have been taken into account for giving stress on the case of ensuring industrial safety referred by safety programs. The programs have included safety education for giving explanation of proper care and attention for taking precaution of the safety of workers.

Initiation For Location of Industrial Set Up

In order to concentrate on employment opportunities, the State Governments have aimed their efforts to grant permission for the initial location under the following aspects namely representatives of Central State Power representative of the department of the State experts in the specified fields, specialised scientists with specific knowledge and representative of the local authorities. These aspects are being taken into consideration during the time of establishing industries for maintaining selection of recruitment possessing qualifications and experience so that they might be counted in period of manufacturing, storing, handling or prescribed works. The other condition is as followed during the recruitment of persons – consideration of age must be maintained with certification of medical and health ground for existing efficiency in work.

In addition to, for the potential Industrial Structure, the Industrial Licensing Policy is used for balanced economic development of different regions in the country so as to reduce disparities in levels of development since every investor needs the clearance from the licensings authorities for finding significant influence or special pattern. But these factors are being decided entirely by the decision of the State. The decision taken by the state is used to play a significant role in altering the special pattern of industries.

These location of public sector plants and special distribution of licenses are used for variables in making assertion of economic policy for the influence of the state on special spread of industries. They pursued for regional dispersal. The persuasion of the policy is used to the state for its satisfaction on the basis of Government's ideological and political objectives. For instance, there were steel mills such as Murmur Gao in Goa, Vellory in Mysore, Bailadilla in M.P. and Vishakhapatnam in Andhra Pradesh – these locations have been selected for industrial locations in achieving political and economic goal. For selection of location as decided factor by the Central Government, the policy is expected to influence the special pattern of private assessment in making enquiry about licenses issued by licensing authorities.

Thus, for analysing the mixed game initiated by our country stressing on industrial set ups for existing on continuation inter-sectoral performance in character. The character is meant for achieving regional equality, Government relied on adhoc committees and working groups. These adhoc bodies evolved for specifying crieteria in making identification of backward regions. For these regions attempts are being made to follow suitable use for developing and the backward regions.

Throughout the planning period of the country, the Government policies were namely based on two specified factors viz; the development of infrastructural facilities for spreading of industrialisation and development of policies evolved for small-scale industries that make a regional balance to the large-scale plants. In view of recruitment of pattern of staffs in this industrialisation process, the Government also looks at the linguistic recognitions of state boundaries resulting for increasing regional pools and pressures.

Further, the Government also gives stress for orientation of market that is meant for role of rationality, public sector investment and wider special spread for achieving regional dispersal.

Thus, keeping in view of mentioned facts the Post-Independence era has made its process of industrialisation by playing dynamism in the process of industrialisation in our country. Such dynamism has been adopted by the Government for adaption of theories of economic development through recruitment of persons in industrialisation for different ranks. This adoption has been meant for reduction of poverty from the country by making a process of determinant for industrialisation process that has occurred in space. The objects of this adaption for creation of typical industries characterising the features of development economies under assumption of finding homogeneity in incomes and the consumption of work in mass.

7

Conclusion and Suggestion

In view of employment opportunity to the Indian Industrialisations there may be stated that at the end of the World War II, Indian economy had registered expansion in manufacturing extracting and service industries. These industries followed diversification of the composition of trade and tax sources of public revenue, allocation of public expenditure in position of tariffs and also the industrialisation of army and social services were enough conditions to bring an amount of national economy. Since the country achieved her independence after World War II. During the period two places, Calcutta and Bombay showed varying characteristic for process of characterisation in the country. The characterisation was completely dependent upon the availability of local merchant and its relative strength in comparison of British capital. Since India achieved her independence in 1947, where a general significance has been understood for changed process of industrialisation. The changes have been brought in new shape to the post Independence economic environment attributing different characteristic such as tariff quotes subsidies taxation investment incentives and the prime object was to give greater attention for employment opportunity to the Indian people. This opportunity of employment provided a new climatic organisations that had to be operated in constituting economic environment undervent significant changes. Changes of post Independence economic environment resulted in application of political and business strategies with formed rules and regulations and were placed in different plans periods of the country in context of mixed economy and federal polity. The mixed economy pattern of administration in the country with the working process contributed the extent role of the country influencing on unemployment problem and moderate market forces emphasising on business policy through market mechanism.

Since after Independence of the country, our late Prime Minister Pandit Jawahar Lal Nehru give his ideologies towards the industrialisation process for welfare of the state. This process referred assessment of material capital and human resources and technical and making application under formulation of policies for effectiveness of utilisation of human resources. The resources determined in mixed economy of the country consisting of defence project, light capital goods industries and consumer goods industries.

Under these application arrangements, the political philosopher as well as beaurocrats thought in creation of diversed industrial sector for absorptions of unemployment youths. The purpose of this absorption was in-operational goal for achieving national income desired investment and imbalanced to remove imbalanced inequalities of income to the people of the country but these goals were mainly concentrated in generation of employment opportunities that were possible for identification of industrialisation concept so the industrialised concept have been put in extended form based on manufacturing industries and their markets. The concept of industries had been analysed concerned with productions in efficient forms for different plan period. In view of healthy climate of plan periods, there can be realised that the Fifth Five-year Plan (1974-79) showed the significance for the national growth and reduction of regional inequalities. The national growth was stressed on national economy where as regional inequalities were meant for emphasising to the problems concerned with unemployment situation in the country because the aims of leaders and beaurocrats were to eliminate reduction of poverty in extended form by an identification of the following indicators; social economic classified sectors and assumption of backwardness. These ingredients characterized the degree of homogeneity of economy among the people of the country.

For stimulated awareness the planners paid their attention for existence of increased trend of income to the people by means of generating employment opportunities in the light of giving suggestions made by planners. They intended to frame certain policies for both organised and unorganised manufacturing industries so that absorption of the persons might be made in extensive form. For formation of extended employment opportunities, the planners had made up there right for selection of location, resources, linkages with materials (raw-materials) and techno-economic and feasibility for creation of industrial operation in terms of greater output to the people.

In maintaining perspective process, the process of development could make successful industrialised economy; forward literal and backward linkages. But all these linkages analysed structural form of employment in generalised industries for creating an unurban environment on the part of exact manifestation of the phenomenon of realistic existence. The existence was completely based on the outputs of manufactured products within the process of industrialisation that required external markets for finding sectoral linkages within national economy. The market economies provided innovated morals that pursued process of social concept of industrialisation approached toward increased external and industrial economies by means of greater opportunities of employment to the unemployed persons.

The main stream of micro economies tend to take care for concerning the special decision in realisation of various factor such as analysed influenced labour cost on the cost of production during the time. But, however, with great endeavour of estimating parameter of specified modals that contributed the aggregate of the problems of variation in cost, the variation in the cost of production. The cost of production explored and pricing sales in maximised forms, combined utility, maximisation, maximization of manageral utility and development all behaviour theories- all these factors brought evolution for an approach of employment opportunity in variety environmental firms concerned with the analysis of nature of work and productivity produced by specified industries.

With advent of productivity in an ideal industrialised process linked with large or small scale of industrial enterprises through stressed respective parameters like; capital investment, generation of output income and employment, profitability of the enterprises and deployment of reinvestment surplus- these factors have been measured to remove poverty as well as unemployment problems contributing toward both rural and urban economies with defined objectives concentrated on the performance of employment situation of the country. The situation indicated manufacturing units of different productivities for absorption of employment of the persons of the country under frame of capital investment (fixed and working capital), generation of output, income and employment etc., depending upon assigned factors such as; identification of beneficiaries raw-materials, finance market labour transport power and technologies etc. The generation of output had been implemented with systematic effort for identification of industrial entrepreneurs emphasising on development of areas covered by the population particularly in their income.

Based on indicated factors the purpose of the author was to know positive actions in promotion of employment intensity. The employment intensity framed elements of strategies policies and programs for intensifying employment intensity of growth related with the activities towards the employment authorities as well as governmental interference. The interference is meant for making justification of growth of employment in different phases subjected to the condition of regulated rules. Thus a long term of employment is that it becomes more and more organised leading to the natural consequences, sign of development awareness of open unemployment situation- all make an aggregate in the generated economy. In fact, underemployment to the organised sector is also recognised as important factor because it particularly converts into more intensive employment and partly in open employment. The open unemployment follows variations from state to state of the country and this variation is found a slow measure of elimination of poverty of the country.

Under employment and disguised unemployment have been remarked as characteristics of under development than any thing else. But its world considering that under employment is also a means of work sharing. It is true at the same time that work sharing in a situation of low productivity, large number of people below poverty line, though at the same time giving them essence of participation in the productivity activities of the society. The participation in the productive activities follows a considerable proportion of people out of work or engaged with work with respect to their income. This approach makes an arrangement of work creation to the developed society.

In the process of creation of employment situation one factor is counted known as waged labourers that are predominant among the sectoral people; i.e. rural or urban sectors. Those features reinforce the inter state distribution of rates of unemployment situations. The technology development also provides an unemployment situation because it scatters skillness and unskillness. In light of these two stated factors there is need to give emphasis on employment elasticity for different plans of the country. But the assumption of an employment elasticity 0.47 for the 8th Five-year Plan is based on a number of policies changes and positive actions to promote employment intensity of development. Observed employment elasticity during the period 1977-78 to 1983 was 0.54 per cent, this decline to 0.38 during 1983 to 1987 to 1988. The decline was noted in respect of sector of the economy including agriculture. But the decline was sharp in manufacturing i.e. from 0.68 in the previous period to 0.26 in the later period. The 8th Plan mixed up to raise employment elasticity in agriculture to 0.5 and that in manufacturing also to 0.5 and aim that corresponding increase employment elasticity of other sectors as well to give an average elasticity of employment to growth as 0.47. For this the Government efforts showed a balanced situation between employment and unemployment situations in terms of loan based resources (energy, water, forest, minerals, environment and ecology). These terms have been highly used in the manufacturing sectors for productive gains.

Inspite of existing these difficulties the long-term trend of technologies and evolution of technologies are found in question. The creation of unemployment is defined as saving of labour expedition of labour that become unsustainable in environmental resources though the trend in technologies has been induced relatively with prices of land base and energy resources. For the reversal process we adopted following in line of production such as engaging the small business attention towards dispersal entrepreneurship and holding for dispersal productive assets. These three factors come under umbrella of organisations or supports of provided technologies infrastructural measures market supposes in the world in decentralised forms.

Summing up these stated factors, the unjustified set provides unemployment situation is the most distributing social problem in the hour present society. It can also be said as the social even and negated forms of human and social development. This negation can be automatically achieved by additional growth of full employment with reoriented structures emphasising saving on land based energy, an environmental resources because these factors will play an important role in the evaluation unemployment problems of the country. They would eliminate disbalances in the alignment of wide spread unemployment and collapsed system in relation to the unemployment situation.

Besides the stated factors there follow some important concept in relation to fiscal human resources and satisfied productivity. These elements operate on inputs processor output and feedback- following goal orientation and achieved certain objectives for a good environment referring for products services information's and ideas to satisfy environment demands. Processor transforms inputs and outputs as exists in a machine or an individual or a computer or chemical equipment. The process of inputs and outputs leads an organisation under the system as a dynamic hole not as a collection of function rather it flows information material and manpower capital equipment and money set up that provides goods services as per demands of the environment (society). The environment comprises external factor over which the organisation and management has little control. This relatively uncontrollable factors are;-

(i) Demography, (ii) Economic Environment, (iii) Social and Cultural Environment, (iv) Political and Local Environment, (v) Technological Environment, (vi) Echology, (vii) Competition and (viii) Demand.

These forces are counted for constituting business under provision of resources and opportunities influencing survival and growth of employment conditions.

But all these factors require an oriented goal for achieving certain objectives in interest of performance profitability they are social cultural. Giving stress on business organisation there is determination of socio-economic system of larger environmental system in finding proper opportunities for changed environment forces. The forces exist in different elements such as changes in outer environment for example, changes in customer demands, changes in market conditions, changes in public relations technologies of these factors are found bounded by dynamic environment expressing for profitable growth or progress. If these elements exists in positive actions, there naturally arises maintenance of balanced increased and growth of employment situations of the country.

Over and above, the marketing system is formed for finding maximisation of life quality in case of consumer goods and services.

Because marketing management formulates an environment to monitor policies and requirements of any enterprises in solution of employment considerations. The elements based on market situations can be explained in the following ways.

(a) Demography: the marketing management is directly interested in demography, i.e. scientific study of human population whose analysis is dealt with quantitative elements for various factors included with elements for various factors included with employment consideration.

(b) Economic environment: this factor is mainly related with the market by which purchasing power and willingness of spending money can be assessed. The purchasing power can indicate the employment situation of any place affecting upon promotion efforts of business units either in positive or inactive forms.

(c) Social and Cultural Environment: These forces usually influence the welfare of a business concern in the long run that may give indicator of employment situation to any society.

(d) Political and Legal forces: these forces consider importance in marketing activities an operation of enterprises following with different policies such as governmental, fiscal import-export and customs. These elements maintain the competition and protect process that influences in framing the trend of employment situation.

(e) Technology: it is one of the important components for consideration of employment situation because it indicates the skillness and unskillness of labour for achieving innovation and development of markets. The innovation products in the market make develop form of employment situation to any civilised society. These dealing in view of aforesaid forces, there can be remarked that positive situation of employment must exist for happiness of the individual to the society incompetent form that requires industrial growth to the country.

The present study consisting of six chapters has dealt with the problem not only absolute shortage of jobs in industrial units of the country but balance in the off-take and the availability. In the context of the study, there has thrown light on the structure of employment opportunity in various industrial units that followed special significance. The significance is commensurate to the growth of job opportunities with increase in supply. The supply of manpower has not been tailored to the needs of dynamic economy, there by resulting in avoidable surplus some others jobs go abegging.

In relation to development approach to employment opportunity, the present system of industrial relations is devoid of economic contents. It is divorced from the realities of the economic world. It prepares industrialised life to the people of the country, without effectively equipping them for it. Here it lies the tragedy what is needed is a revolution in thinking - a revolution in employment policy which should take full cognizance of the change that is sweeping the economic and commercial life. Those who want to earn their livelihood in urban areas should be taught what is relevant and practical in urban life.

In this regard, the first chapter performed three periods viz. initiation of reforms, rapid growth and period of slow-down, in examination of 1989 to 1999 into three distinct parts. Also regions of the country have been classified with increased, decreased and stable employment opportunities to persons for distinct periods in terms of percent variation (table 1.1). The percent of variation in employment opportunity classified employment opportunity that has understood and regulated socio-economic changes following with the relationship between economic growth, poverty and unemployment. The relationship between these three factors contributed an evidence of growth in employment in organised industry, private and public sectors since 1973 – 97 (table 1.2) followed by the following:

(a) Change in the size structure,

(b) Capital intensive and labour intensive, and

(c) Relative share of the size class and income in the relative share.

These growths of employment opportunity contributed significanty employment in key industries since 1995 in case of four classified industries (Table 1.4-1.7).

There has also been pointed out in achieving balanced results in cases of production and employment to different classified industries of the country by quantifying and qualifying labour supply-purely economic impasse, labour absorbing potential and responses of appropriate and proportionate existed technologies employing possible indicators dealt with statistical measures.

The second chapter of the study has provided growth rate of employment in industrial sectors that tended to take view of various measures of labour, capital, source of income, direct consumption by producers of industrial sectors (small and medium industries). In finding characterisations of increase in money wages, wage–price flexibility in the market etc. These factors have been undertaken into consideration of difference between the consumption standards of the employed and unemployed persons. This study also provided parameters involved in the volume and incidence of unemployment and differentiation between wage and the value of marginal product of available labour or labour force participation in various industrial entreprenureships based with great deal of comparative studies. Each of these factors has been exhaustively interpreted by considering different components, e.g. profit bonus, general bonus, higher wage rate, periphery benefits or extended welfare programmes. Such determination of factors coinciding with labour productivity in growth rate of employment - the capital - labour ratio, the relative factor pirces i.e., capital labour ratio, the relative factor prices i.e. wages in relation to the cost of capital costs in consideration of level of technology. In this consideration, a 'sub-system' of money, profits and prices has been used for opportunities of higher returns on capital in unlawful trades like smuggling, black marketing, hoarding and illegitimate speculation based on institutional dimensions indicating market barriers financial structure availability of credit and other factors that made indication of optimum output. Further there has been estimated of 'unemployment and its trend' by making study of NSS data and also censuses of 1981 and 1991 summarised in different tables of given subject for both organised and unorganised sectors having stratification of capital investment, expenditure for present rapid investment, expenditure for present rapid economic growth.

Because, in time of economic expansion it provides a steady growth of expenditure more or less similar to the growth in national prosperity. For financial purpose, it facilates the preparation of accounts in which expenditure is clearly demarcated making it possible, in theory, to observe trends in the scheme more closely.

In this way, a discussion has been laid for cases of availability of credit, the wage gap governing the return margin on capital and current rate of growth of economy as well as market barrier.

In relation to the rate of growth of employment there has been explained 'sub-system', of money, profits and prices levels for finding concrete shape of analysis of the demographic, social and economic background with recommendation for the introduction of social security in formation of administrative or accounting methods with the assistance in the planing and organisational services.

Also there have been explained for place of employment development, plan, technical index of performance as well as the strategy for itergenerational equity which required the need for realisation of employment to the man population. In this context the author could conceive on degree of employment or non-employment characterising of efficiency in production on assumption of labour force introducing demand and consumption of goods at substantial measure that created employment policy. This study enabled us to make investigation of the feature of enterepreneurship for both government and non-government organisation prevailing of consumption of goods with equitable distribution to workers in the present mordernised industrial phase calling indicator of equitable growth expansion of industrial inverse and objective of the employment and fast pace of industrial production.

In addition, employment condition for welfare of the society has been enlighted with presentation of neo-classical analysis that made increased or decreased trend of employment conditions. This study has been done by making frame hypothesis based on wage rates, wage paid employment, capital expenditure and national income etc. These studies have been done numerically and by the presentation of facts in numerical number. There resulted various interpretation concerned with employment opportunities through industrial process in India, where size of the population, stock of capital and rate of growth and other factors have been extensively discussed with presentation of statistical tables since 1950 covering employment opportunities for different states of the country. It means labour force proportion to the population of different areas have been interpreted in extended form as given in table 2.2 corresponding to different manufacture products.

The chapter third has given light on extended industrial process in the country usually meant for standardised by the ILO through conventions of employment opportunity to persons in various individuals. For this sake there have been several recommendations for technical co-operation, formulated programmes, enacted and implemented rules and regulations based on the principles of employers in identification new benefits, innovative benefit provisions, nationalisation and simplification of existing schemes as controlled and regulated by the organisations and institutions of industrial relations.

In this relation, the study could provide an emphasis on the process of industrial relations for which clarification of Mandays, use of labour of the country, labour intensive technique, proportion of workforce, expanded scheme of employment, current employment at the highest levels, substantial growth of development in industrial concerns, tentative decision of initial benefits from entrepreneurship, etc.

The chapter third 'Evolution of extended industrial process in the country' revealed studies based on labour policy and certain social economic and political conditions envisaged by the Government of India to implement in the principle of Industrial democracy in different states of the country. This study required statistical process to analyse data since 1971 to 1985 that followed different statistical tables, particularly stressing on the principles laid on different plan periods. In this context the author attained a statistical table of employment condition corresponding to specified industrial sectors since 1979 to 1985 to have knowledge of trend based on Sixth Plan Period.

Further, the author could be able to evaluate overall employment to the organised sectors and also to give stress on percentage change in employment. Thus, the statistical table – 3.7 provided employment generation between First Plan Period to Fifth Plan Period. In this way growth of net-national out-put based on inudstrial process has been evaluated by assumption of net-national product and annual growth plan. The author has also contributed capital investment and employment consideration for First Five Plan Period were employment generation has been shown in terms of percentage of million to overall states of the country as figured in table 3.9.

But their implementation has been vitiated by technical and administrative deficiencies and corruption on a phenomenal scale. (These have been documented in some recent work). Therefore it is highly unlikely that the theoretical possibility of eradicating the bulk of recorded unemployment and poverty by the century will really be actualized. Unless the poor are universally coincides and unionised to demand the actual delivery of the promised productive assets, guaranteed wage employment at poverty-line income, infrastructure and social services, without inefficiency and misappropriation.

Thus, there has been formed a conclusion that under the influence of different applied models, occupational psychologists tended to believe for management and workers. So that management might gradually learn the proper provision for the peculiar characteristics of human machine paid off in terms of worker's contentment and efficiency and appreciation of job satisfaction and their recognition. Because the workers possess certain values, goals and capacities which follow under the following sub-systems, viz; (a) the technological system (including technology and physical work environment), (b) administrative system (including supervision, formal organisation, etc.) (c) workers (including immediate workgroup, other workers), and (d) union (staff association and professional association).

The chapter four has dealt with performance of the objective of the study that has explained attributes of employment generation skillness the workers to unvested capitals in industrial sectors. Because the influence of established industrial relations implicits contributed management to give due consideration to conflict to integrate where interaction is led with other dimension in the historical process. In this connection, the objective of the study has also stressed non-skilled workers in different instrumental of labour, to assess proficiency in assertion of employment opportunity. The same chapter proceeded level investment as guide lines to the industrial enterpreneureship for developing situation of the country under different programmes. This study has also indicated that the unemployment depressing phase of expanded development. The objective of the present study indicated a justification that caught the imagination of experimental social psychology under any sort of social management. Undoubtedly, economic & political explanations required definite psychological applications that may have political & economic consequences but under the limitation of industrialisation. But in view of examining these facts this study required to give emphasis on poverty alleviation and employment generation. The picture for expanded employment opportunity concerned with agriculture industrial relation followed by direct & indirect effects of modern manufacturing in different proportion. In addition to, the purpose of this study has thrown a light on achieved equity to workers under miserable conditions who were affected by two more components namely unemployment and poverty.

Further, the objective of the study analysed dynamic economy of the country referring growth rate of employment. In this relation their necessiated wage profit relation, cost of capital goods, determination of level of technology, institutional base, governing the production relation and incentives following composition of level of output. In spite of dealing all these components there required in determination of market barriers for availability, location and illegitimate speculation to have an acquaintance of velocity of money evolved in different enterprises of the country. Such objective has also given provision of stratified formation of capital investment of self-employment in expanded, effective ways to absorb an employment conditions prevailing in the country for a long period. Such prevailing situations in the country required to contribute an adequate measure of evaluation of employment condition of the country.

The chapter five has dealt with the study of employment that was caused by industrial sickness. Though, the Indian Political system is committed to develop industrial units for achieving some of the socialistic objectives mentioning equitable distribution of wealth balance regional growth, creation of employment opportunities, etc. The last fact is considered more potent but existing of industrial sickness, there arises unemployment situation in the country. In this connection, the mentioned chapter anaylsed data based on NSSO under constraint of both sex male and female, sector rural and urban and also considerable districts. Proportion of relevant data have been estimated for these constraints. The sudden spurt in the number of sick units has been received to the Government and public for giving proper attention. But the unchequered growth of sickness of industrial units could not be properly solved for the reason of availability of raw materials, power, transport and working finance facilities, of marketing the product, Government distribution system and attitude of the financing institutions. These factors in industrial units have made misallocation of manpower and created serious problems of budgetary deficit and disguised unemployment amongst nationals.

Though, recent development in psychology of personality and motivation has promised to be of some real use in improving our understanding of entrepreneurial behaviour. Therefore the present study has made stress on variables achievement, motivation, risk bearing properesity job anxiety, need for power, work value, leadership style and level of aspiration.

Many institutions and organisations, obscenely to bring about economic growth, may not be aware of the key role entrepreneurs play in realising the organisation goal. Therefore, the study has reflected entrepreneurial orientations by means of training programmes to promote entreprenurial behaviour.

The chapter six followed characterizations of structural changes accompanied with industrialisation for production process counting its important constituents such as cost of the service of resources, value added by necessary labour & value added by surplus labour denoted by C. V & S respectively. This study provided information about adequacy of employment generation in various dimensions for industrial structure of the country. In this regard, to reach the level of production the most important quotients have been used such as abolition of feudal production, increased formation of agricultural sectors, reduction of exploitation of the common people and nationalisation of foreign companies for dynamic economy of the country. These quotients provided broad conceptual measure of geographical factors, development of productive process, division of labour and level of per capita income. These components made an indication of occupational distribution of working population of the country since 1901-1991 referring censuses of India. The percentage of variation in different sectors, the tended values of different success changed activities in proportion of workforce of the country and compared increased, decreased and stable trend between grants of employment & population of the country. In light of these studies historical evidences have been determined categorised form of employer's organisation of the country that carried out different activities formed by employers and employees of the industrial sectors. This elaborate study followed widened and expanded industrial environment by giving different instances under industrialised legislative conditions.

Finally, the study reached in taps of subjective complex & transient norms for having essence of industrial organisation – a regular standardised and recurrent behaviour following regular functions normative as well as structural implications.

Bibliography

Ahluwalia, I.J., Op. Cit.

Baner, Indian Economic Policy & Development.

Banerjee Ramadev, Journal of Development Economics, 1980.

Birla Agreement with Communist State Govt. in Kerala on labour matter. Approaches to education and manpower planning.

Bishwanath Goldar (2000) "Employment Growth in Organised Manufacturing in India",

EPW Mumbai vol.35, no. 14, April, pp 1191-95.

Chakraborty, S., Policy making is mixed economy. The Indian Case in P.R.

Brahmananda & V.R. Panchamukhi (eds.). The development process of Indian economy (Mumbai, 1987)

C.N. Vakil & P.R. Brahmanand, c.f., planning for a shortage economy.

Casseor, R.H., Indian population, Economic Policy in India (Poone, 1972)

Datta Chaudhry, Mrinal (1995) : "Labour Market as Institutions in India", working paper no. 16, Centre for development economics, Delhi school of economics.

Draft Fifth Plan (1974-79), Planning Commission, Government of India.

Draft Five Year Plan (1978-83), Government of India, New Delhi, 1978, p.82.

'Easter Economist', Annual Number, 1980. Golden, B.N. Product.

Gadgil, D.R., Planning & Economic Policy of India (Poone, 1972)

Govt. of India, Ministry of Labour Bureau, Rural Labour Inquiry, 1963-65, Final Report.

Govt. of India, Planning Commission, Sixth Five Year Plan, 1980-85.

Govt. of India, Ministry of Finance, Direct Taxes Inquiry Committee, Final Report, Delhi, 1971 (Non-coal 1985).

Govt. of India, Ministry of Labour, Statistics of Mines in India, Vol. II.

Gupta K.P., Agricultural Labour in Jalan District (U.P.) An Economic Survey, Pd.D. Thesis, 1981. Ibid.

Hellinger, S.H & D.A. Hallinger (1976) : "Unemployment and the multinationals - a strategy for technological change in Latin America, London, pp. 3-8.

I.L.O. – Recent Development in certain aspects of India Economy – IV. James Riedel,

Industrial Employment Expansion under Alternative Trade Strategies; Case of India and Taiwan, 1950-1970.

Jain P.C. Planning in India.

Kuznets Simon – Economic Growth and Structure – Selected Essays (Now Delhi, 1945)

Kuznets S., Towards a Theory of Economic Growth in R. Lakachman.

Krishna K.L., Op. Cit.

Khan M.Y., Op. Cit.

Lucas, Robert. E.B. (1988) : India's Industrial Policy in Robert E.B.Lucas and Gustav

Papanek (eds) The Indian Economy. Recent Developments and future prospect, Oxford University Press, Delhi.

Montek S. Ahluwalia, Growth and Poverty in Developing Countries.

Mathur C.F. A.J. & J.S. – Op. Cit., Page – 256.

Nagraj, R (2000) : "Organised Manufacturing Employment", EPW, Vol. 35, no. 38

Mumbai, pp 3445-48.

Nicolas G. Garter, Journal of Development of Economics 6 No. 3 (Sept. 1979).

Patel Surendra J., India's Regression in the World Economy, Economic Political Weekly, Sept. 1979).

Popla, T.S (1994): "Structural Adjustment, Labour Market Flexibility and Employment"

Indian Journal of Labour Economics, Vol. 37, no. 1 January - March, pp 3-16.

Prasad Kamte, Employment Potential of Selected Manufacturing Industries in U.P., ICSSR.

Public Enterprises as Employer are not included in the discussion.

Rao, V.R.R.V., India's National Income 1950-80 (New Delhi, 1983).

Rao, Rammohan, Op. Cit.

Seventh Five Year Plan, 1985-90

Sixth Five Year Plan.

Sen A.K., "Economic Approaches to Education and Manpower Planning", Indian

Economic Review, New Series, Vol. 1, 1966.

Silver Jubilee Souvenir, P.15.

Singh B.K. & Singh B.P., Op. Cit. P.276

Singh, M (1993) : "New Economic Policy and Challenges before the Labour Economics" inaugural address to the 34th conference of the Indian Society of Labour Economics, Vol. 36 no. 1

Sixth Five Year Plan (1980-85). Govt. of India, Planning Commission. The Hindustan Times, Patna, July, 97.

The world Bank, World Bank Report, 1984 (New Delhi, 1984).

World Bank, World Bank Report, 1988.

Index